PUPIL PROFILES

PUPIL PROFILES

A Guide to Understanding and Teaching Children and Youth

by
Roger C. Reeds

A textbook of the
Sunday School Workers' Training Course

VOLUME III

Randall House Publications
114 Bush Road — P. O. Box 17306
Nashville, Tennessee 37217
1973

Textbooks in this certificate series

Volume   I   ORGANIZING AND DEVELOPING A
                  SUNDAY SCHOOL
Volume   II   COMMISSIONED TO COMMUNICATE
Volume   III   PUPIL PROFILES
Volume   IV   DISCIPLING AND DEVELOPING
Volume   V   FAITH FOR TODAY

PREFACE

This volume, *Pupil Profiles*, is the third in a series of five designed to serve as a Sunday School Worker's Training Course.

This particular volume sets forth the various characteristics of the age levels that are commonly assigned to the Sunday school. The teacher is directed through the chapters as strata of rocks. Each chapter compliments the other.

In addition the teacher will be able to glean pertinent information as to how to better perform his responsibility. Every teacher needs a knowledge of teaching techniques, methodology, Sunday school organization, and soul-winning techniques. There is a little of all of this in this volume.

I have drawn upon my years of experience as a pastor and as Director of the Sunday School Department. I am indebted to so many who have made contributions to the book. Most of all I am indebted to my faithful wife, Myrtle, who has worked with me through these years. Her work has complemented mine. I dedicate this book to her as she has dedicated her life to serving the Lord and me.

Yours for greater Sunday schools,
Roger C. Reeds

Requirements for Credit When Studying This Volume in Class

  I The course may be taught by the pastor or someone whom he recommends.

 II A minimum of 45 minutes for each chapter must be spent in classroom instruction.

III The pupil must have read the textbook.

IV The pupil must attend at least 2/3 of the class sessions.

  V The instructor shall give the pupil some form of written work. This work shall be evaluated by the instructor.

VI A list of the names of those successfully completing the study shall be sent to the Sunday School Department, P.O. Box 17306, Nashville, Tennessee 37217. Credit cards will be processed through this Department and forwarded to the instructor for signature. The name of the volume studied shall be given.

How To Earn Home Study Credit

  I The text must have been read.

 II All of the questions at the end of each chapter must be answered on paper. These questions should be checked and approved by the pastor or Sunday School Superintendent.

III Make a request to the Sunday School Department for a credit card. This request should certify that the text has been read and that paper work has been satisfactorily completed.

INTRODUCTION

Amos Bronson Alcott once remarked, "That is a good book which is opened with expectation and closed in profit." The book that you have in your hand is such "a good book." For the teacher who desires to know his Sunday school pupils and to teach them well, this book can be profitable indeed.

Reverend Roger C. Reeds is well qualified to write this book. After thirteen years in actual Sunday school work while serving as a pastor, Mr. Reeds assumed the position of director of the fledgling Sunday School Department in 1961. Since that time he has led that Department in a development program almost unparalleled in religious circles.

The basic purpose of the book is to acquaint teachers with the general characteristics of pupils at the various age levels. The author has gone beyond this and has incorporated references to methods of teaching which will allow the teacher to view his work in a much broader perspective.

"The books that help you the most are those which make you think the most" is a true saying. Mr. Reeds' book will have achieved its goal of being profitable to the teacher as it challenges him to a greater study of his pupils. Through a greater knowledge of his pupils will come a broader impartation of knowledge. Open this book with expectation and I believe you will close it with profit.

J. D. O'Donnell

CONTENTS

Prologue 9
Chapter 1
The Cradle Roll Child 17
Chapter 2
The Nursery Child 34
Chapter 3
The Preschool Child 54
Chapter 4
The Primary Child 77
Chapter 5
The Junior Child 103
Chapter 6
The Junior High Youth 124
Chapter 7
The Senior High Youth 151
Chapter 8
The Young Adult 175
Epilogue 199

PROLOGUE

A truly fascinating verse of Scripture is found in Romans 9:20.

"Nay but, O man, who art thou that repliest against God? Shall the thing formed say to him that formed it, Why hast thou made me thus?"

Unquestionably we are "the thing formed" or the by-product of creation. We are marvelously made. We live in an environment that is marvelously made. We were made to be the master of our environment but instead our environment has become our master.

Man has come to the place that he questions his creation as well as his Creator. He is willing to accept someone's theory as to his origin rather than believe the fact of creation. Consider the following facts: The normal man has 245 bones, 446 muscles, 1,000 ligaments, 4,000 lacteals and lymphatics, 10,000 nerves, 100,000 glands and over 200 million pores. All of these working parts are controlled by a mass of grayish tissue that weighs three pounds. It is called the brain. Individually, the parts of the body function in an amazing fashion, but collectively, as they work in harmony, their function is all the more stupendous. The only just conclusion to arrive at is that man is the greatest invention the world has ever known, fashioned by the Greatest of all inventors.

Time and time again man has asked the question, "Why hast thou made me thus?" This book shall attempt to answer this question. We already know that we are the result of two factors . . . our heredity and our environment. Psychologists are at odds as to which factor contributes the most to the end product.

It was God who created the first man and the first woman, but since this initial act of creation man and woman have united with God in procreation. The parents of every offspring make a strong contribution to their child in both heredity and environment. It is stated in *Man and His Biological World*, "Although a great deal remains to be discovered about heredity, yet within the past forty years much has been learned regarding that process which is of inestimable value to both the scientist and the layman."[1] We will give some attention to this idea of heredity in the next several paragraphs.

Every species has a number of highly effective structures which transmit the hereditary influences from parent to offspring. These hereditary influences are called *chromosomes*. Each human being has forty-eight chromosomes. Half of these forty-eight chromosomes come to the child from his father, the other half from his mother. It is known that within each of the chromosomes a child receives from each parent are many still smaller parts called *genes*. These genes are microscopic in size and carry the real determiners of heredity. The whole heredity of the individual consists of many traits, each determined by a gene, a pair of genes, or a group of genes.

In lower organisms it is possible to determine by carefully conducted experiments the exact chromosome and gene involved in the hereditary transmission of a particular trait. In man, however, the process is so complex that there is little hope of accomplishing a similar result. Most human traits are apparently determined by a large number of genes.

We all know that there are often striking resemblances between parents and children, and between children of the same parents. Yet, we also know that there are often striking differences among parents and offsprings and between the offsprings of the same parents. This difference is brought about because some genes are recessive while others are dominant. This aspect of genes is too broad to be discussed here but it should be sufficient to point out that genes may contribute to likeness or difference in heredity.

Lester D. and Alice Crow report the following interesting information in *Readings in Child and Adolescent Psychology.*

A popular misunderstanding of the functioning of biological inheritance is evidenced by laymen who speak of a child's inheriting a characteristic from his mother or father. Studies in this field have given us the following principle: 50 per cent of a child's characteristics probably are inherited from the mother's line and the other 50 per cent from the father's. It has been estimated further that one half of a child's native characteristics are inherited from his parents, one-fourth from his grandparents, one-eighth from his great-grandparents, and the lesser fractions in proportion down the ancestral line. These relationships between inherited traits and family potentials can explain some of the differences that are found in siblings.[2]

It is time now to depart from the discussion of heredity and turn to the influence of environment upon the offspring. Everyone lives in an environment—by which we mean the external surroundings of man. Man cannot live in an environment without a response to his environment. If this were possible then man would live in a vacuum and be nothing more than a vegetable, however, even a vegetable responds to environment. The color of the vegetable as well as other traits may be inherited but the size and vitamin potential of the vegetable is influenced by such outside influences as the soil and fertilization.

Man never ceases to be influenced by his environment. The parts of the environment that make man react at any particular moment give off "stimuli." The word *stimuli* is the plural of *stimulus*, which in Latin means "goad." In psychology the word stimulus refers to some form of physical energy which, if it were sufficiently intense, or if the change in its intensity were strong enough, would arouse nerve impulses from those cells.

The importance of the environment and its influence on the individual is discussed by Floyd L. Ruch, Professor of Psychology at the University of Southern California:

> An individual could not exist or develop except in an environment, and must depend on his environment for the means of satisfying his basic needs for food, warmth, and so on. Every individual has a complex relationship with his environment, because he is complex, and because the environment itself is complex—containing not merely the means for physical sustenance but also people and social institutions which mold the individual in certain habits, desires, and interests known as the "social motives." For example: the average American requires both food to keep alive (a biological need) and also a feeling that he is "getting ahead in the world" (a social need). But whether the environment is physical or social, the individual is always interacting with it in many complex ways.[3]

An important characteristic of human nature is the inherent ability to respond to stimulation in such ways as to bring about changes in attitudes and overt behavior. From the time an individual is born he has the power to learn. It is thought that the strongest influence of environment takes place in the first six years of a child's life. During this period the child is guided by his elders into specific kinds of learning. Certain habits are developed without the child being overtly aware of them.

Every child matures in an environment that is peculiar to itself. Several studies have been made of the effects upon the child of the culture in which he is reared. Psychologists are in agreement that children all over the world are similar in their growth and maturational pattern. The differences that exist in the behavior of children reared in different cultures would be the result of the cultures themselves.[4]

The responses to the stimulation of one's environment are called adjustments. These fall into two categories—unlearned and learned responses. Unlearned responses are those in which man has no opportunity to influence or modify his action by past experience. Unlearned responses may involve instinctive action or simple reflex action. Learned responses involve all aspects of conscious, intelligent reaction. One of the interesting and valuable aspects of learned responses is that they may become habitual. At first an act initiated by a stimulus requires elaborate, deliberate, and laboriously formed connections before it can emerge in the form of a response, but once the whole train of procedure has been accomplished, the act is slightly easier to do a second time.[5]

It is time now to relate our discussion with that of teaching a Sunday school scholar. By the time we receive the scholar under our influence he has become rather well molded. He has come under the influence of his heredity and environment. There is nothing we can do about a child's heredity. It would help us though to better understand the child if we did know something of the child's background. In many instances the child has already come under the environmental influences of the home and the school before he comes under the influence of the Sunday school teacher. Even if the child begins in the Cradle Roll Department, the Sunday school teacher only has a limited sphere of influence over the child.

The role of the Sunday school teacher is not a simple one, though some teachers approach it as such. He must become the *stimulus object* in the classroom. We have observed that a child learns as he responds to stimuli. A light bulb is a stimulus object, but the light it gives which enters the eye is stimuli. The Sunday school teacher is to teach the Bible which he recognizes as the stimuli that can change lives. As the stimulus object he is to encourage learned responses in the lives of the pupils in his class. These pupils may be children or they may be adults, but as human beings they will respond to stimuli. The wise Sunday school teacher will recognize the influences from inside and outside that help to mold the individual's life.

The chapters that follow in this book will help Sunday school teachers to recognize and understand the generalities that are known about their scholars. In addition there are various helps and suggestions for the teacher. The teacher discovers who his pupil is and where he is and uses the necessary tools of his trade to lead the pupil to Christ and the higher planes of spiritual life.

---

1 Frank Covert Jean and others, *Man and His Biological World* (Boston, 1944), p. 487.

2 Lester D. Crow and Alice Crow, eds., *Readings In Child And Adolescent Psychology* (New York, 1965), pp. 41-42.

3 Floyd L. Ruch, *Psychology and Life* (Chicago, 1948), pp. 9-10.

4 Crow and Crow, pp. 44-46.

5 Jean and others, pp. 187-193.

THE CRADLE ROLL CHILD

The Cradle Roll child is that child who is enrolled in the Cradle Roll Department of the Sunday school. This rather simple definition introduces the ministry of the Cradle Roll Department as well as the child who falls into this category.

The earliest record of a cradle roll dates back to 1880. A small boy dropped one penny into the birthday bank in a Sunday school in Elizabeth, New Jersey. He acknowledged that the penny was not for himself but for his baby brother who was "too young to come to Sunday school." The boy's teachers decided to compile a list of other babies too young to attend Sunday school. This early beginning evolved into a dangling list of names on cardboard cradles. For many churches this list gathers dust as a very vital ministry is overlooked.

The ministry of the Cradle Roll Department can be two-fold. It can become the source of reaching parents with the gospel message. The parents of a new-born baby have tender hearts. The experience of childbirth has put them in touch with God as they have joined Him in procreation. The Cradle Roll ministry reaches out to parents and babies who are unchurched as well as those parents who are saved and members of the church. This particular ministry is of special value in reaching the unchurched. They may be discovered in a variety of methods. To discover prospects for the Cradle Roll

Department one might follow these suggestions:

1. Compile a list of prospective babies from your own church.

2. Search for prospects among the friends and relatives of the members of your church.

3. Watch for birth announcements in the newspapers and on hospital lists.

4. Watch the neighborhood clotheslines and diaper service trucks.

The second aspect of the Cradle Roll ministry involves the baby himself. In many instances he is completely overlooked as an effort is made to win the parents. In other instances he is brought to church and placed in a situation that is nothing more than glorified baby-sitting. Some people reason that a child cannot learn much in these early years. Psychologists have proven this theory wrong.

WHO IS THE CRADLE ROLL CHILD?

The Cradle Roll child is less than two years of age. Normally he is enrolled in the Cradle Roll Department immediately after birth. He may or may not be brought to Sunday school. He has been thrust into an environment that may or may not be a Christian environment. He is at that stage of life where he will learn more than he will ever learn in all of the rest of his life.

There are some who prefer to think of the Cradle Roll child as being anywhere between birth and three years of age. Those who do so look upon the Cradle Roll Department as only a home ministry. With this approach the child is transferred to the Nursery Department when he is brought to Sunday school. He remains there until he is old enough for the Kindergarten or Preschool Department. It has been found that the learning capabilities of the 2-and 3-year-old child are so much more advanced than a child who is younger that it is best to have a separate department for them. What previously was one department has now become two. They are:

> Cradle Roll Department — Birth — 2
> Nursery Department — 2—3

Because the capabilities of the Nursery child are so much more advanced they will be discussed in the next chapter.

THE CRADLE ROLL CHILD AT HOME

In the home aspect of the Cradle Roll ministry the emphasis is placed upon the parents. The very fact that the child is not brought to church would indicate that the parents are not Christians. Contact is made by the Cradle Roll workers who are missionaries in the truest sense of the word. These workers visit the homes, show a keen interest in the infant members of the families, and tactfully try to establish a close bond between parents and the Sunday school. Some other purposes of the Cradle Roll workers are listed by the late Dr. Bernice Cory, who was editorial director of the Children's Division of Scripture Press:

> To leave literature with the parents.
> To establish a continuing contact with the parents that will win them to Christ or attract indifferent Christian parents back to the Lord.
> To help parents realize that their baby is a gift from God.
> To help parents to understand their role in Christian nurture.
> To encourage family devotions.
> To encourage regular attendance at Sunday school and church.[1]

The ultimate goal of the Cradle Roll worker then is to win the unsaved parents to Christ and to encourage them to become regular in church attendance. The by-product of these parental decisions for Christ will be the changed environment at home for the offspring as well as the fact that the child is now more than just a name on the cradle roll. The child can now be brought to church where he may begin his process of learning from the Bible. He may continue this process through the remainder of his life. He will neither complete nor exhaust the study of the Scriptures. He will never graduate and receive a diploma from the Sunday school. The Cradle Roll child who is brought to church is embarking upon a life-long program of study. He is totally unaware of this fact as he begins to learn about and from the world that surrounds him. The Cradle Roll worker can assist the Cradle Roll child in learning that it is God's world and that he is God's creation.

THE CRADLE ROLL CHILD AT CHURCH

It is Sunday morning. A young father stops his automobile at the curbstone in front of the church. He hurries around the automobile to open the door for his wife. She is holding a bundle engulfed in a blanket. The young man assists the woman up the stairs and into the church. She handles the small parcel gingerly. The two appear to be slightly nervous and unsure as to direction. A knowing usher steps forward and greets the young couple and guides them to the Cradle Roll Department. They hesitate and seem reluctant to surrender their new month-old child to the arms of the attendant. After assuring themselves that their child will be well cared for they move on to their own classroom.

The young parents are fortunate in finding a

church which provides competent attendants for their baby, as well as feeding, sleeping, and playing facilities. Dr. Cory believes that adequate space for the Cradle Roll Department is necessary. She says,

> It is not optional nowadays but practically mandatory that a church wanting to grow, provide well-equipped rooms for babies, preferably in charge of a registered or practical nurse, on duty through both Sunday school and worship service. If this is not possible an experienced mother may take charge. She will need enough helpers to feed and care for the babies—one for each five or six. These attendants may serve on a rotating basis, so that they can take turns attending church. A young father may also be a great help, especially with the older babies who often respond more readily to a man than a woman.
>
> As each baby is brought in, his feeding and sleeping schedule should be written down and his bottles labeled with his name on adhesive tape. Toddlers' helpers may be more than baby-sitters. They can help the older babies to appreciate God's creation, love, and care with books, games, visuals, and action play.[2]

Dr. Cory has struck upon a very important fact that is often ignored by many. There is no time as fruitful in laying the groundwork for a rich spiritual life as during a baby's highly impressionable years.

THE CHARACTERISTICS
OF THE CRADLE ROLL CHILD

The development of a child is extremely rapid throughout babyhood to the age of three years. To realize how rapidly the changes occur, all one has to do is compare a three-year-old child with a newborn infant. The development is continuous from birth to death, but occurs at different rates—sometimes slowly and sometimes rapidly. Because development is continuous, what happens at one stage has an influence on the following stage. Emotional tension in the home will affect the young child's development in personality and will be reflected in personality scars later in life.[3]

Genetic studies of babies from birth to age two have shown that there is a general behavioral pattern that all babies follow. This pattern is as follows:

From 4 to 16 weeks, the baby gains control of his 12 oculomotor muscles. (These control the movement of the eyes.)

From 16 to 28 weeks, he gains command of

the muscles which support his head and move his arms. He then begins to reach for things.

From 28 to 40 weeks, he gains control of his trunk and hands. This enables him to sit and to grasp, transfer, and manipulate objects.

From 40 to 52 weeks, he extends control to his legs and feet, to his forefinger and thumb. He can now stand upright, poke and pluck.

During the second year, he walks and runs; articulates words and phrases; achieves bowel and bladder control; and acquires a rudimentary sense of personal identity and of personal possession.[4]

The Baby's First Year. As one surveys the chart listed above one can note the marked change in the advancement during the first and second years of the baby. These years have been labeled as *babyhood* by psychologists. Because of the vast differences in the one-year-old and two-year-old child, we shall observe their characteristics separately.

Adults are always ogling over a child and asking, "What is going on in their little heads?" when inspecting a new baby. Since we cannot recall our own experience at that age and since the baby cannot tell us what he is "thinking about" we are left without much information. The truth of the matter is that the child is probably thinking very little. He has not learned to focus his eyes as yet so he cannot learn by using them. The neonate (a child who is from two to four weeks old) relies heavily upon the sense of touch, and will learn to rely upon the other receptors (senses) as he progresses in growth. The neonate's needs are relatively simple. He needs to be fed, made comfortable, and loved. The Cradle Roll worker can assist in supplying these early needs of a new baby.

It is uncertain as to what emotional responses the newborn infant is capable. Certain child psychologists once believed that the emotional responses of the newborn infant were of three specific types: fear, anger and love. Later research has failed to bear this out and indicates that the emotional life of a newborn child is more general. Emotion that could be termed general excitement is aroused by internal stimulation, such as hunger, as well as by external conditions, such as temperature changes and physical stimulation of various types.[5]

The infant begins a process of sensory-motor development. Part of this development is inherited and part of it is learned. It becomes difficult to separate the two. Once the child has learned to focus his eyes he can begin to learn by association. He learns to associate the various sensations of warmth, touch, and taste with the visual sensation of his mother. One of the early evidences of sensory-motor development is the smile, which occurs by about the second or third month. This response is social and is triggered by the appearance of the mother or some other person or some inanimate object that is moved in the line of the infant's vision.

Before the end of the first year the infant can respond to the oral speech of other persons. It is recommended that even new born babies be "talked to." There is no need to use the imitative baby talk that adults are prone to use when talking to babies. In the first six months the infant will make some attempt to talk back to his adult companion. The sounds will only be cooing and babbling but they help to stimulate the infant. Notice how his excitement seems to peak as he babbles. Sometime during the 6- to 9-month period the infant will begin to imitate and duplicate sounds he has heard others make. These sounds are parroted though as the child has not learned to associate words with objects. By the time he is 11 or 12 months old he may be able to identify "Mama" and "Dada" and call them such. The year old infant may be expected to have one or two words in his vocabulary. He is now ready to depart from his comfortable Sunday school room of cribs and rockers and move in with the toddlers. As he has learned to speak his first few words he has at the same time learned to use his arms and legs to become mobile. At first he crawled or creeped but now he is taking some unsteady steps.

The Second Year. Several things will be noticed about the progress of a child in his second year. For one thing, he continues his rapid rate of growth. His muscles are developing and he is a tireless rover. It is in error to say that he is tireless for he will tire rapidly and require sleep throughout the day. The Cradle Roll worker should allow some period of the Sunday school hour for a rest period. It may be that the child will fall asleep and sleep through the worship service as well, but these long sleeping periods are normal.

By the time the child is 18 months old the walking behavior is pretty well under control as it becomes an automatic habit. His vocabulary has increased to the extent that he may use a single word to express a complete thought. McCarthy notes that the toddler may mean, "There is the ball," or he may mean, "Where is the ball?" or, "I want the ball" when he uses the simple word "ball." Some psychologists have observed an increase from 3 words at 12 months, to 19 words at 15 months, to 22 words at 18 months, to 118 words at 21 months, to 272 words at 24 months. In the last three months of the second year the child begins to combine words to form larger segments of thought. By 24 months he is capable of using simple phrases and sentences.[6]

THE BEGINNING OF THE EGO

Another very important aspect of development occurs during this second year. It is the beginning of the development of the child as a separate individual. You have recognized his separate identity, his parents have recognized the child as a "self," but the child grows into this self-identity.

The newborn infant does not differentiate himself psychologically from his mother. He does not conceive of himself as a person and certainly not as a person who is separate from other persons. When he has a need, that need is readily met by his mother and so he cannot separate himself and his needs from his mother. As he grows and learns to do things for himself (especially feeding himself), he begins to develop the idea of a self-identity. Before long he recognizes himself in the mirror as a distinct personage. He finds there is a difference between "me" and "mine" and "you" and "yours."

THE CHILD AS A SOCIAL BEING

Social behavior begins in the child when he first learns to distinguish between persons and objects. His first social responses are to adults because his first social contacts are with adults. By the end of the second month, the baby turns his head when he hears a human voice. He expresses pleasure in the presence of others by kicking, smiling, and waving his arms. By the third month the baby will recognize his mother and other familiar people. He will stop crying when talked to and cry when a person leaves him. In the fourth month the baby will laugh when he is played with. In the fifth and sixth month he will react differently to smiling and scolding. He distinguishes between friendly and angry voices. By the eighth or ninth month the baby will attempt to imitate speech sounds as well as simple acts and gestures observed in others. By the end of twelve months the baby has learned to refrain in response to "no-no."

From the fifteenth month on, the baby shows an increasing interest in adults and a strong desire to be with them and imitate them. At two years, he can cooperate with adults in a number of routine activities. [7]

TEACHING THE CRADLE ROLL CHILD

Very little can be taught to the Cradle Roll child during his first year. This does not mean he is not learning, because he began to learn the very moment he was born. The Cradle Roll worker will have the responsibility of supplying the love and rendering the necessary body care requirements so as to make the child comfortable.

By the time the baby is ready to join the toddlers in their big, spacious quarters, he is ready to embark upon some learning adventures. These will be limited but they can be meaningful. The games the child plays can have some teaching value. Building blocks, balls and other expressive toys can carry pictures of animals and birds and the child can be told that God made these animals and birds.

When the child has reached 18 months he will enjoy someone reading to him. Simple books that contain more pictures than words are readily available. There are many fine Bible picture story books that are prepared with the small child in mind. The older Cradle Roll child will enjoy things such as action and finger play. Since he is already acquainted with dolls or teddy bears he will enjoy being talked to by a hand puppet. The puppet might even be some kind of an animal.

The older Cradle Roll child is ready to learn that there is a God, that He is in Heaven, and that He loves him. He will not understand all he is told about these concepts but he can be told. He can be taught to pray although he will not understand prayer and his praying will be imitative. The Cradle Roll child can begin to learn an appreciation for the church building as God's house. He can be started on the road to respect the furniture in God's house as well as the building itself.

THE CRADLE ROLL CHILD
IN RETROSPECT

To summarize the previous pages we will again call upon the writings of Dr. Cory,

The Cradle Roll Department of the Sunday school is gradually being recognized as an outstanding service agency. For no other department in a well-functioning Sunday school so effectually links church and home and brings entire families into the Sunday school and church. The Cradle Roll is the foundation of the Sunday school, for it starts where life itself starts—at birth—and maintains interest in a baby till he is two and is "promoted" to the nursery department.[8]

The Cradle Roll worker should keep in mind that every baby is an individual. The worker can become acquainted with the generalities of the characteristics of children from birth through age 2, but the worker should also become acquainted with each child individually. The worker should know the kind of background that the child is from so that he can help meet the basic needs of each individual child. This fact is true no matter what age level is taught.

It is evident that some of the best trained and most highly skilled workers in the Sunday school will be needed on this level as well as the next several levels.

These are the foundation years and if the foundation is weak surely the building will collapse as it ages and suffers the ravages of time.

CHAPTER ONE

FOOTNOTES

[1] J. Edward Hakes, ed., *An Introduction to Evangelical Christian Education* (Chicago, 1970), p. 125.

[2] *Ibid.*, p. 130.

[3] Elizabeth B. Hurlock, *Child Development* (New York, 1964), pp. 18-19.

[4] *Ibid.*, p. 121.

[5] D. Bruce Gardner, *Development in Early Childhood* (New York, 1964), pp. 90-91.

[6] Dorothea McCarthy, "Language Development in Children," in L. Carmichael, (ed.), *Manual of Child Psychology* (New York, 1954), pp. 492-630.

[7] Hurlock, pp. 336-337.

[8] Hakes, p. 123.

CHAPTER ONE

QUESTIONS FOR REVIEW

1. What is the two-fold advantage of the Cradle Roll ministry?
2. Who is the Cradle Roll child?
3. How can one discover prospects for the Cradle Roll Department?
4. What is the ultimate goal of the Cradle Roll worker who visits the new baby at home?
5. It is stated that it is best to have two separate quarters at church for the Cradle Roll Department. Why?
6. Describe the characteristics and needs of the Cradle Roll child during his first year.
7. Describe the characteristics and needs of the Cradle Roll child during his second year.
8. Is it possible to spend a great deal of time in teaching the Cradle Roll child during his first year? His second year?
9. Is it valuable to know each member of the Cradle Roll Department individually?

CHAPTER TWO

THE NURSERY CHILD

The Bible gives only a limited view of Jesus as a child. One verse of Scripture does give us a keen insight into the early development of Jesus, especially in light of today's knowledge of child development. Luke 2:52 tells us about the early growth of Jesus in a broad sweep, "And Jesus increased in wisdom and stature, and in favour with God and man." This verse presents four areas of growth in the life of our Lord. He grew physically, mentally, socially and spiritually. All children pass through these same stages of growth.

THE PATTERNS OF GROWTH

Physically. We have observed in the previous chapter that the first several years of a child's life are years of rapid growth. The rapid growth in the first year necessitates two sets of clothing, the infant size for the first 6 months and the first size for the last 6 months. The next larger size is usually adequate for the child until his second birthday. He then settles down into a growth pattern that is so universal that his clothing can be sized accordingly.

It is necessary that we know the growth norms as we prepare our Sunday school environment for our twos and threes. Hurlock tells us that there is a pattern of growth which is similar for all children. She provides the following averages:

The child measures—

At birth	—19-20 inches
At four months	—23-24 inches
At eight months	—26-28 inches
At one year	—28-30 inches
At two years	—32-34 inches
At five years	—Double his birth height

The child weighs—

At birth	—6-8 pounds
At four months	—12-16 pounds
At one year	—18-24 pounds
At five years	—30-40 pounds[1]

The child enters his first stage of slow growth when he leaves babyhood (age 2) and enters childhood (ages 2-11). He will maintain this slow steady pace of growth until he reaches puberty. At that time the second stage of rapid growth begins.

The typical 2-year-old American child weighs about 27 pounds and is about 34 inches tall. The typical three year old weighs about 32 pounds and is nearly 38 inches tall. There is not a great deal of difference in size between boys and girls during this period, although the boys do tend to weigh slightly heavier. Because the child has moved into the period of slow growth there is typically a lessening in appetite and accompanying lack of interest in food.[2]

The basic nature of the Nursery child's growing physical body demands an almost continuous flow of activity. There is an innate urge to make use of the muscle systems, which are gradually being brought under control. The Nursery child's steady list of physical activity, which naturally tends to emphasize the large muscular action involved in gross body activities, contributes to muscular development and coordination.

Motor development is the gradual process of bringing the skeletal (voluntary) muscles under volitional control. From the very beginning of life, motor behavior plays a part in the child's perception and awareness of his world. Motor behavior is also essential for the child's development of speech. Vocal activity itself is motor behavior.[3] The teacher of this age level must keep in mind that the Nursery child has only gained control of his gross movements which involve movements of the large areas used in walking, running, swimming, and bicycling. He will not gain control of the finer coordinations which involve the smaller muscle groups used in grasping, throwing and catching balls, writing or using tools until after five years of age.

The Nursery teacher should realize that his pupils need motor activity. The well-equipped Nursery Department will provide outlets for this need. The motivation for the activity comes from within the child; the provision for such activity must be made. Motor activity helps the child form an opinion of himself. His success or failure image is being established at this early age. *It is a wise teacher, as well as parents, who magnifies the successes and minimizes the failures.*

The Nursery child will learn basically by the use of his hand skills as well as through his vocabulary. The Nursery teacher should be acquainted with both. Hurlock lists the norms for hand skills:

The two-year-old—
—can open boxes,
—unscrew lids from bottles or jars,
—turn the leaves of a book,
—build a tower of four or five blocks,
—insert a circle, square, or triangle in a form board,
—scribble with pencil or crayon,
—string beads,
—smear paint,
—roll clay,
—drive a nail into soap or soft wood,
—cut a gash in paper with scissors.

The three-year-old—
—can undress, wash, and feed himself,
—can dry dishes,
—can carry a tray,
—can string four beads in 2 minutes,

—can build a bridge of three blocks in the imitation of a model,
    —can copy a circle in the imitation of a model,
    —can cover a picture with paint or crayons.[4]

As the child moves into his second year his vocabulary begins a rapid expansion. Imitation is the basis of this rapid expansion. Gardner provides the following scale of vocabulary growth:

2 years	—272 words
2 years, 6 months	—446 words
3 years	—896 words
3 years, 6 months	—1,222 words [5]

The speech sounds of a two- or three-year-old may be difficult to understand because of poor articulation. The competent Nursery teacher develops skill in comprehension of this ariticulation as well as skill in communicating with the Nursery child.

Mentally. As we have noted in the previous chapter the new-born child has the capacity to think but lacks the ability to do so. Most of the child's early responses are reflex in nature. The outstanding tools of learning for the young child are the senses. He is under constant stimulation by sensations. None of these sensations become meaningful in the child's thinking process until his vocabulary has been built. For example, when precisely can a child tell what is meant by the word *cold?* He must first experience a certain sensation caused by contact with ice, cold water, or cold air. When his vocabulary has been built far enough to include the word *cold* he learns to associate the word with the sensation.[6]

We must not reach a conclusion that the child can only learn through the sense of touch. He will learn from the other senses as well, for they are used individually and in harmony with one another. Still another factor is important in the process of learning and that is the role of motor behavior. Motor behavior coupled with sensory processes contributes strongly to learning.

Our old friends, *heredity* and *environment*, contribute to a child's mental development. The exact role of heredity in producing the mental development of the child is not known. There does seem to be sufficient evidence that genetic factors do contribute much to a child's learning ability. Additional evidence points out quite clearly that environmental factors can smother any genetic factors that may have contributed to a child's development. Growth studies conducted by psychologists have shown that children who were deprived of normal mothering experiences were adversely affected in mental growth as well as in other aspects of development. If maternal deprivation continued over a significant period during infancy, the trend toward inferior mental development became irreversible.[7]

If a child has his early learning experiences through the senses then he can only learn that which is concrete or that which is perceived by the senses. Abstract thinking will come later in his childhood. For example, object lessons would be meaningless to the Nursery child.

As the child's world is broadened, his learning ability is extended. He learns by imitation and can be seen copying what others do. He cannot discern between good and bad and thus will imitate both. For example, the teacher may wish to teach the Nursery child about kindness. Merely telling the child to be kind means nothing to him, but as he sees another's kindness, he, too, wants to be kind.

The Nursery child learns by asking questions. He is curious about his world and wants to know about it. He believes anything he is told. Teachers should not discourage children from asking questions. The teacher may not know the answer at the moment. He should admit his ignorance frankly and promise to find the answer as soon as possible. The teacher should keep that promise. If a child is taught something that he discovers to be untrue later he will come to doubt the things that are true.[8]

From our survey of the mental ability of the Nursery child we can conclude a few things about the child. He has limited concepts of time, space, and number; a short interest span; sensory curiosity; limited vocabulary; and a lack of experience. Trained workers are needed to adjust Biblical teaching to these demands and to make Bible stories relevant to the small child's experience. Songs and Bible verses must pass the same test of being literal and simple.[9]

Socially. How a child develops socially will depend a great deal upon his cultural heritage. For instance, there is a good deal of difference in the social expectancy of the American child and that of the French child. To say that Jesus "increased . . . in favour with man" does not cast Him in the same light socially as the American child. Jesus was an Israelite and was raised socially in the culture of the Israelites. If one has read even slightly he has learned that there is a marked difference between western (occidental) and eastern (oriental) culture. Since the child is the by-product of his environment he will adopt the social customs of his environment.

Americans are very much concerned about the social behavior of their children. The word social is defined as having to do with human beings living together as a group in a situation requiring that they have dealings with one another. Thus we Americans are concerned that our children should learn to play and mingle well and cooperatively with other children. We emphasize, for example, that the child learn to share, to wait his turn, to be considerate of the needs and feelings of others, and in general to be liked by others.[10]

No child is born social or antisocial. What the child's attitudes toward people and social experiences will be and how he will get along with other people will depend largely upon learning experiences during the early, formative years of his life. These experiences will, in turn, depend upon the opportunities he has for socializing, upon his motivation to take advantage of these opportunities, and upon the direction and guidance he receives from parents, teachers, and older children in the best methods of making social contacts. Should all of these factors, which play so important a role in his learning, be favorable, the chances are that he will develop into a social person. Should they be unfavorable the chances are great that he may become antisocial.[11]

As someone has said, "socialization does not proceed in a vacuum." The child who has had experience in the Cradle Roll Department has been started on the road to socialization although he is not ready to become a social being. At least he has been weaned from his mother and has accepted his teacher as another adult human being.

If a two- or three-year-old attends the Nursery Department for his first experience in Sunday school he may prove to be difficult for the first several Sundays until he is weaned away from his mother. This could well be his first adventure into socialization. Once the child has become convinced that the teacher too is a human being, and that his mother will indeed return for him at the end of the Sunday school hour, he can safely turn his attention first to play materials and then to the other children.

Young, Nursery children may treat each other like mere things to begin with. Their first play is likely to be of the parallel variety, that is, they play alongside rather than with other children. The children at first find it very hard to talk to each other except in imperatives, negatives, and possessives ("Don't!", "No!", and "Mine!").

Studies of groups of children have revealed that, while the two-year-old is solitary in his play, he is nevertheless influenced by older children to the extent that he imitates their behavior both in his play activities and in his conduct. The 2½-year-old child grabs toys from other children and refuses to share them; he ignores requests and refuses to comply. However, by the time the child reaches three years of age he shows the beginnings of team play.

One of the many advantages of the Nursery Department is that it provides social experiences under the guidance of trained teachers who promote enjoyable contacts and are on the alert to see that no child is subjected to treatment that might condition him to avoid social contacts.

Spiritually. Elizabeth Hurlock discusses the religious interests of a child in her book titled *Child Development,*

> Religion includes two elements: belief and practice. Both are important throughout life, but at different ages the relative importance of each varies. The younger the child, the greater his interest in religious practices. Interest in religious beliefs is slower in developing because it depends upon the intellectual development of the child; the younger the child, the less able he is to comprehend the meaning of religious beliefs.
>
> The child's interest in religion is fostered by the training he receives in the home, Sunday school, or church and by the emphasis placed on religious observances in his daily life. The child who has a home environment in which grace is said before every meal, who is expected to say his prayers before going to bed, and who has parents who read or tell him stories from the Bible will have a greater interest in religion than the child whose main contact with religion is his weekly visit to Sunday school.[12]

We have already noted that the Nursery child is curious by nature. Regardless of the religious instruction he receives, the child is curious about the heavens above him which produce rain, snow and sunshine. He is curious about the everyday world. Between the ages of three and four years the child's questions often relate to religion. "Who is God?" "Where is Heaven?" "How do you get there?" The child accepts almost any answer he gets.

Bible stories will appeal to the child in much the same way as fairy stories. Both relate to people, countries, and situations so different from those of the child's everyday environment that he enjoys hearing them over and over. At different ages different parts of the Bible will appeal to children. Nursery children will prefer stories relating to the birth and childhood of Jesus as well as the childhood of such Bible characters as Samuel, Moses, Joseph, and David. These children are interested in persons and happenings, not doctrines.

The Nursery child can learn to pray but most of his prayers are said in a somewhat parrot-like fashion. He can be taught the common grace prayer . . .

> God is great, God is good,
> Let us thank Him for our food.

. . . or the common bedtime prayer . . .

> Now I lay me down to sleep,
> I pray thee, Lord, my soul to keep.

If I should die before I wake,
I pray thee, Lord, my soul to take.
If I should live for other days,
I pray thee, Lord, to guide my ways.

. . . but these prayers will only be mechanical to the Nursery child and will tax his ability to memorize. Even though the prayers of the Nursery child are parroted or mechanical the fact of prayer can be established in his life. The chances are that if his prayer is not memorized and he is allowed to pray "out of his heart" most of his prayers will involve "give me's" rather than "thank you's."

Stewardship training can be started on the Nursery level. The Nursery Department teacher will find that the Nursery child is not a "cheerful giver." He has learned the power of possession and many times will cling to the coin and proclaim, "Mine!" With proper patience the teacher can begin the child on the road to giving. As he sees the teacher and others give he will want to give. Important lessons of stewardship can be implanted in the Nursery child's mind. The ministry of giving should be made an important part of any Nursery worship program. The child should not be told that he is giving his money to Jesus for he knows he is placing his money in a box and cannot understand how it will get to Jesus. He can understand that the money will be used to buy things for the church such as the book he uses in his Sunday school class.

THE NURSERY CHILD
IN RETROSPECT

We have observed that as the Nursery child leaves babyhood and enters childhood his rate of growth is slackened. The child is prodded into continuous action by an inner urge. The Nursery teacher might command her 2's and 3's to "sit still!" but this is an impossible task for them. His large muscles are developing and crave action. He appears tireless but tires quickly.

The child's vocabulary expands by leaps and bounds in years two and three. The Nursery teacher needs to develop an understanding of the language of the Nursery child if she wishes to communicate with him.

The Nursery child likes repetition and will not mind hearing the same stories over and over again. He is likely to have a favorite book that he wants read to him repeatedly. Usually the stories will have to be brief for his attention span is short.

The Nursery child will believe everything he hears. Television has already captured his imagination and he readily accepts whatever he sees and hears on his favorite program. He does not understand symbolism so parables and proverbs are meaningless to him or they could provide him with a false conception. He obtains a great deal of his information by asking questions as he attempts to satisfy his insatiable curiosity.

The Nursery child is not ready to socialize. He will

play alongside other children rather than with them. This is especially true of the two-year-old child. During his third year he will begin to show signs of "warming up" to other children.

Every child is born with an interest in religion. He has a natural vacuum in his life that can only be filled with the spiritual. This does not mean that he will be ready to receive Christ during his Nursery years. This decision will be reserved for the Beginner or Primary years. If not by then surely during the Junior years. Seeds can be sown during these early years that can be cultivated and brought to fruition in later years.

THE NURSERY TEACHER

Every aspect of our discussion thus far has been directed toward understanding the Nursery child. For the next several paragraphs we shall turn our attention toward the teacher of this level or levels as well as to the classroom setting. It is difficult to avoid digressing from our main purpose for this presentation which is to set forth the profile of the pupil as he progresses through the various levels provided for him in the Sunday school.

Some dear lady approaches the pastor or Sunday school superintendent and says, "I would like to teach a Sunday school class. Since I've not had any training or experience I think I would prefer to work with the little ones." In too many instances this request is granted. We have learned that the child who is two or three is in some of his most formative years. If the teacher is to accomplish her task she must be qualified to do more than baby-sit with the children and keep them quiet during the Sunday school hour.

The trained teacher can make Sunday school a vital, interesting hour for the Nursery child. If possible the two's should be separated from the three's. In no other department of the Sunday school is it so necessary to work with individuals as it is in the Nursery Department. You should have gained some insight as to how to teach the Nursery child by reading through this chapter and learning something of his characteristics. The wise teacher will secure additional books and read more widely on the subject. The bibliography that appears at the end of this book will provide you with a suggested list of books to read. Many of these are secular but they will provide a good insight into the characteristics of the Nursery child.

The teacher must keep in mind that no one can rightly describe every child who is two or three. These characteristics that are provided in this chapter are the norms or averages which are arrived at by testing groups of children. There are always exceptions to the rules. Getting to know your pupils individually will help you understand them better. You can equate them to the

norms and see wherein they differ and adjust accordingly.

PHYSICAL SURROUNDINGS
AND EQUIPMENT

If clothing factories are able to size clothing to fit children ages two and three then surely we can furnish a classroom setting that will meet their needs. Dr. Mary Le Bar, professor of Christian Education at Wheaton College makes some good suggestions about educational facilities for the Nursery child.

To achieve the kind of teaching indicated requires an environment set up
specifically for the young child. Allocation of
space should follow the rule, "the smaller the
child, the more space," rather than the
inverted idea often followed by church boards
in planning. Choice locations for health conditions, including cleanliness, light, ventilation
and even heat, on the first floor should be
given the small children. Materials for teaching
are not necessarily large, but they are sturdy
and manageable by hands or feet that are as
yet incompletely coordinated.[13]

The classroom should be equipped for teaching through play as well as structured for teaching. The equipment that is provided will be suited to the height of the Nursery child. All equipment as well as materials should be durable for their durability will be tested by the pupils. Any handwork that is provided should be simple. Crayons should be large. Scissors for this and all lower levels should be blunt ended and not too sharp. Some visuals such as the General Electric Show'N Tell can be used. Most of the Bible programs that are available are about four minutes in length and will run the length of the Nursery child's attention span. Bible pictures, simple flannelgraph, and hand puppets will catch and hold the child's attention briefly. An interest center such as a sand box which depicts some Bible scene such as baby Moses in the basket boat can be constructed.

CONCLUSION

The Nursery teacher with a sanctified imagination and a sincere desire to communicate can be used of God to touch young lives. Some churches have used men in the Nursery Department to project the father image at church as well as at home. The church that wishes to accomplish God's purpose will make adequate provision for the foundation years. To fail to do so is not only failing God but the lives of the young children of the community.

CHAPTER TWO

FOOTNOTES

[1] Elizabeth B. Hurlock, *Child Development Fourth Edition* (New York, 1964), p. 120.

[2] D. Bruce Gardner, *Development In Early Childhood* (New York, 1964), pp. 122-132.

[3] *Ibid.*, pp. 147—148.

[4] Hurlock, p. 192.

[5] Gardner, p. 176.

[6] Marie L. Avery and Alice Higgins, *Help Your Child Learn How to Learn* (New Jersey, 1962), p. 4.

[7] Gardner, pp. 211-214.

[8] Marjorie Elaine Soderholm, *Understanding the Pupil, Part I, The Preschool Child* (Grand Rapids, 1958), p. 28.

[9] J. Edward Hakes, ed., *An Introduction to Evangelical Christian Education* (Chicago, 1970), p. 137.

[10] Gardner, p. 287.

[11] Hurlock, pp. 326—327.

[12] *Ibid.*, p. 600.

[13] Hakes, p. 143.

CHAPTER TWO

QUESTIONS FOR REVIEW

1. Who is the Nursery child?

2. Why is it important to know about the physical characteristics of the Nursery child?

3. Does a wholesome environment contribute to the Nursery child's mental development?

4. Name at least three ways that a Nursery child learns.

5. Can the Nursery Department contribute to the social growth of a child? If so, how?

6. Is the Nursery child ready for any spiritual attainment? Be ready to discuss your answer.

7. Will the Nursery child's prayer life be meaningful? If your answer is yes, then how? If your answer is no, then why?

8. It is not necessary to place the best trained teachers in the Nursery Department.

The above statement is true or false. Be ready to support your answer.

CHAPTER THREE

THE PRESCHOOL CHILD

The four- and five-year-old child has been given several titles. For years he was known as a *Beginner* although this title becomes difficult to explain. The child has already gone through many beginning stages so one cannot rightly call him a beginner. Some have preferred to call him *The Kindergarten Child.* This title is associated with the idea that the five-year-old child is given some taste of public school prior to his entering first grade at age six. This early experience in education has been called Kindergarten, a German word that means literally—a garden of children. More recently the four- and five-year-old child has been called a *Preschooler.* Of course this name could appropriately be given to any child between infancy and the school age. Since this title is the latest in vogue and probably the best known today we shall call our fours and fives—Preschoolers.

GROWTH NORMS OF THE PRESCHOOLER

We should keep in mind that the growth rate of the Preschooler is moving at a slow, steady pace and will continue to do so until he reaches puberty. The typical four-year-old will weigh about 36½ pounds; at age five he will weigh around 41½ pounds. The four-year-old will measure some 40.5 inches in length; at age five he will be about 43 inches long. Fewer than 3 percent of Preschool children will be less than 40 inches tall and fewer than 3 percent of Preschoolers will measure more than 47 inches tall. As a result of this average growth pattern classroom settings can be designed to meet the needs of the highest percentage of pupils.[1]

The typical change occurring during the preschool period is a lengthening-out process as the child emerges from babyhood into true childhood. The child takes on a leaner appearance. His muscles begin to tone. This is accounted for by the incessant activity and natural exercise of the healthy child during the preschool period.

Muscle fibers are present in the child's body even before birth. During the preschool period the growth of muscle tissue is nearly proportioned to the total increase of body weight. Muscles contribute between one-fourth and one-third of body weight during the preschool years. The Preschool child's muscular system is composed of water (about 72 percent) and solids (about 28 percent). The muscles are not yet as firmly attached structurally to the skeletal system as they will be in the years that follow. These factors contribute to the Preschooler's tiring easily and his need of adequate rest periods during the day as well as sufficient sleep at night.[2]

Since the Preschooler craves activity the wise

Sunday school teacher will provide activities for him. The classroom needs to be large enough to allow the children to be mobile. The classroom *must* not be overcrowded. Each room will need an average of 25 square feet for each child. Each room should have no more than 15 pupils and contain at least 375 square feet of space. There should be one teacher for each five to seven children. Team teaching is probably most effective for this age level. More will be said about equipping the classroom later.

Motor Activities of the Preschooler. "I can do it," is a phrase often stated by the Preschooler. He likes to do things for himself. He has learned to dress himself by the time he is five years old with the exception of tying his shoes. The reason the four-and five-year-old child can achieve so well is the further development of control over body action involving the voluntary muscles.

We can refer to our old friend *Environment* as a contributor to motor development. Children in rural districts have the opportunity to acquire more skills in climbing than children in urban communities. The Sunday school teacher should be aware of the fact that children differ in motor abilities. This difference can be attributed to heritage as well as environment. It is true that there are "norms" or averages that the teacher may use as a measuring stick but not every child will measure up to the norms in every sense. Under no circumstances should a child be scolded because his motor activities are slower than the rest of the children. Instead the plodder must be encouraged and complimented for his achievement.

Marjorie Soderholm discusses the use of the large (voluntary) muscles,

> Because he (the Preschooler) does not yet have control of his finer muscles, his handwork should be limited to activities which can be performed by the large muscles. Any pictures for the Beginner to color should be large and free from detail. He should be given large crayons to use, and he may occasionally break one of them because of his lack of muscular coordination. His teacher should be careful not to scold him for something he did not mean to do.
>
> He can hold a pair of scissors properly, but he should be given only those with a blunt edge, for he does not have full control over them. This is obvious when he tries to follow a line as he cuts. He weaves from one side of the line to another. He may even cut off a very important part of the picture—the hand or even the head of the shepherd.[3]

The Preschool child cannot be expected to write. At age four he may be able to print a few capital letters. These will be large and irregular and will usually be the initials of his first and last name. The five-year-old may be able to print his entire name in large, irregular letters. He will frequently reverse his letters. The Sunday school teacher does not have the responsibility of teaching graphology but she needs to know that the Preschool child is not yet ready to use the finer coordination that writing requires.

Vocabulary of Preschoolers. In the previous chapter we noted the rapid progress of the Nursery child in his vocabulary growth. The Preschooler broadens his vocabulary as his world broadens. He has learned that he can use his language to communicate with others. Once more we will refer to Gardner's scale of vocabulary growth:

4 years	1,540 words
4 years, 6 months	1,870 words
5 years	2,072 words
5 years, 6 months	2,289 words[4]

The child may not use every word in his vocabulary but he will understand their meaning. The Sunday school teacher should listen and learn to speak in a vocabulary the child can understand. Failure to do so is to violate one of the Seven Laws of Teaching. These Seven Laws are discussed by John Milton Gregory in *The Seven Laws of Teaching*. Doctor Gregory lists the third law as the law of the language. It is—*The language used in teaching must be common to teacher and learner.* Doctor Gregory lists some of the following rules for the teacher to follow regarding the use of vocabulary:

1. Study constantly and carefully the language of the pupils.
2. Express yourself as far as possible in the language of your pupils.
3. Use the simplest and the fewest words that will express your meaning.
4. Use short sentences of the simplest construction.
5. Explain the meaning of the words by illustrations (objects and pictures are to be prepared for young children).
6. Test frequently the pupil's understanding of the words that he uses.[5]

The use of a proper vocabulary was recognized by the Apostle Paul as he wrote, "So likewise ye, except ye utter by the tongue words easy to be understood, how shall it be known what is spoken? for ye shall speak into the air" (1 Corinthians 14:9).

MENTAL PATTERNS OF PRESCHOOLERS

The mental capacity of the Preschooler will only broaden slightly as he moves up the chronological ladder through ages 4 and 5. He asked questions as a Nursery child; he will ask even more questions as a Preschooler. Perhaps the greatest area of mental expansion for the Preschooler is his curiosity. The trained Sunday school teacher can utilize this extreme curiosity to greater learning advantages.

The Preschooler wants to know how things work. He may take one of his favorite toys apart just to discover the inner workings of that toy. He does not consider the fact that he has destroyed his favorite toy; he is pleased because he has satisfied his curiosity.

The Preschooler's Imagination. The Preschooler has an active imagination. He loves stories in which the bunnies, kittens, and dogs talk to each other. One of the outstanding characteristics of the young child's perception is that which is called *Animism,* or the tendency to ascribe consciousness to inert objects. Children's stories tell of toys and animals that are able to think and feel as people do. Animal cartoons are extremely popular with young children. Perhaps a child will become angry and kick a chair. The mother is likely to say, "Poor chair, you hurt him. Go and tell him you are sorry." Adults tend to encourage animism among children. Some animism is even carried over into adulthood. This is evidenced in the comic strip—Peanuts—where Snoopy, the beaglehound, is humanized.

Hurlock states that there are four successive stages in the animistic concepts of young children,

> In the first stage when children are four to six years old, everything that is in any way active is regarded as conscious, even though it is stationary. In the second stage, between the ages of six and seven years, consciousness is attributed only to things that can move. The sun and a bicycle are regarded as conscious, while a table and a stove are not. Between the ages of eight and ten, in the third stage, the child makes an essential distinction between movement that is due to the object itself and movement that is introduced by an outside agent. Bodies that can move of their own accord, such as the sun or the wind, are looked upon as conscious, while objects that receive their movement from without, such as bicycles, are regarded devoid of consciousness. In the fourth and final stage, which begins at the age of eleven years consciousness is restricted to plants and animals, or to animals alone.[6]

The Preschooler's vivid imagination is one of God's choicest gifts to them and is a great asset to learning. One of the greatest methods of teaching the Preschooler is the story. (It allows the teacher to work the pupil's imagination.) Stories help to frame abstract ideas into concrete ones. The greatest example of the greatest of all storytellers is the Lord Jesus. He could paint verbal portraits that came alive.

There are four requirements to good story telling. A good story should be interesting. One of the best sources of good stories is the Bible. The teacher should be careful to point out that the source of the story is God's Book. It will be natural to say, "I am reminded of a lovely story that is found in God's Book." Or, "I want to tell you a story that Jesus told. We find it right here in God's Book."

The second prerequisite for a good story is that it be dramatic. A good dramatic story will possess conflict, plot, and suspense. Many Bible stories meet this standard. The teacher will have to practice in order to become a good story teller. Do not be embarrassed to practice at home before a mirror. Proper gestures and facial expressions are important. The vocabulary that is used in the narrative must be that which Preschoolers can, understand. Use short sentences. Overwork verbs and avoid adjectives.

A story should be full of action. A good example of an action-packed story is that of the Good Samaritan found in Luke 10:30-37. Jesus did not take time to describe His characters in the story but we learn something about each character by his deeds.

The fourth standard of a good story is that it must be true to life. Every story may not be true (they may be fictional) but they should be true to life. Fairy Tales and fantasies may help to develop the child's imagination but they have no place in the Sunday school hour.

The Sunday school teacher may even use the child's natural attribute toward animism in telling a story. The story teller could become an animal puppet worn upon the hand of the teacher.

The Preschooler's Idea of Time And Space. Every parent is aware of a child's impatience with the passing of time. That birthday or that Christmas holiday just never seems to arrive. The young child finds it quite difficult to understand the time patterns of his society. One child was heard insisting, "It is not today! My mommy said it was Monday!"

The Preschooler will have real difficulty in understanding the yesterday-today-tomorrow sequence. One child said, "I had my birthday last week" when his birthday had been several months past. Last week to the Preschooler may mean anytime in the past just as "tomorrow" may mean anytime in the future. The Preschooler will find it difficult to understand that Jesus lived several thousand years ago or that some Old

Testament stories occurred as much as four thousand years ago.

The Preschooler will have little sense regarding the cardinal directions. North, South, East, and West mean very little to him. He cannot judge great distances. To speak of a Bible land far, far away could bring the image of several city blocks to his mind. To him this is far, far away.

The Preschooler does not know the value of money. Money becomes meaningful to a child only when he has the opportunity to use it. At five years of age, children begin to understand that money has to do with buying, though they do not understand that specific coins must be used for buying different things. The Preschooler can be taught to give his money to the Lord. Good stewardship practices established early in life will result in good stewardship practices later in life.

The Preschooler's Ability to Mimic. The Preschooler has not just learned to imitate others for he has been an imitator all of his very young life. Most of his emotional responses were learned by imitation. Many of his motor responses were learned by imitation.

The Preschool child identifies very strongly with the powerful people in his world. A boy, for example, identifies strongly with his father, for to him his father is powerful and wise. Similarly, a girl tends to identify with her mother and in the process takes upon herself many of the qualities and characteristics, mannerisms, ways of speech, facial expressions, gestures, body postures, etc., of her mother.

As the child's social contacts expand so does his imitation. He will imitate his peers. Observe the Preschooler who is brought to Sunday school for the first time. He will not know how to act or react until he has had the opportunity to observe the other children and imitate them.

The Sunday school teacher may be surprised to learn that the Preschooler imitates him. He may try to retell the Bible story just as the teacher told it using the same mannerisms as the teacher. This imitative ability can be put to work in the classroom. Why not let the child retell the story you have just told? His peers will enjoy it and it will help implant the truths of the story in the minds of the class.

Role playing can be used effectively as a method of teaching because of the child's imitative ability. He will enjoy "acting out" the part of one of the Bible characters of the Bible story.

The Sunday school teacher comes to realize the seriousness of the task of teaching as he observes the child imitating him. Many of the child's life values are learned by imitation. The child will become in later life what he has learned and observed in his early life. That is why these years are called the foundation years.

THE PRESCHOOLER'S SOCIAL CONTACTS

From ages two to six years, the child develops into a distinctly socialized individual. He learns to adapt himself to others and to cooperate in group play activities. These years are often called the "pre-gang age"—the time when the child is normally learning how to make social contact and get along with people outside the home, especially children of his own age. The number of contacts the child has with other children during the pre-gang period is an important factor in determining how far his social development will progress. The *kind* of social experiences the child has is more important than the number. If he has had pleasant contacts with other children or adults outside the home, even though they were only occasional, he usually wants to repeat them. If he has had primarily unpleasant contacts, he will shun further contacts, even when they are readily available.[7]

The real test of a good Preschool Sunday school teacher is the product she or he produces. Has your Preschooler enjoyed a good social atmosphere in his class? If he has he will *want* to attend his class every Sunday. His desire to do so indicates the teacher is successful in establishing a wholesome social atmosphere.

In any group of Preschoolers one can readily observe a variety of social attitudes. There is the "bossy" child who likes to issue orders, to scold, or to protect. He usually comes from a home where his ego is repressed. Occasionally there will be a child who likes to "show off." This springs from a desire to attract attention. Other children in the class may like to follow the "show off" by imitation. Some children come from a happy home environment where grown-ups and children work and share and have good times together. These children usually show the highest of social attitudes, *cooperation.* They cooperate with other children as well as with the teacher.[8]

The Preschool teacher should remember that the Preschooler prefers the approval of adults rather than that of his peers. This attitude will change in the years that follow especially near puberty and the onset of adolescence. The wise teacher will take advantage of this characteristic of the Preschooler and offer his approval often. No one child should be singled out to be praised more than another. The child should be taught that doing right not only pleases the teacher but also pleases God.

THE PRESCHOOLER AND SPIRITUAL GROWTH

"How old must a child be before he can be converted?" is a question often asked. Spurgeon once said, "A child of five, if properly instructed, can as truly believe and be regenerated as any adult." Most of us are aware of the following verses of Scripture:

> Matthew 18:14 "Even so it is not the will of your Father which is in heaven, that one of these little ones should perish."
>
> Matthew 19:13-15 "Then were there brought unto him little children, that he should put his hands on them, and pray: and the disciples rebuked them. But Jesus said, Suffer little children, and forbid them not, to come unto me: for of such is the kingdom of heaven. And he laid his hands on them, and departed thence."

There is no established age of accountability. There are those who baptize infants and others who set the age of accountability at puberty, but one cannot determine this vital milestone in a person's life by one's chronological age. The age of accountability is a term that means the child has reached the mental capability of realizing that he is a sinner; he is lost, and he needs Christ as his Savior. It is a mental age rather than a chronological age. Not every four- or five-year-old child is ready to be saved; however, some are! The Preschool Sunday school teacher *must* be prepared to lead these little ones to the Savior.

Marjorie Soderholm lists several do's and don't's in her booklet titled, *Explaining Salvation To Children.*

Space will allow us a few lines to list some of the do's.

1. The teacher should be clear in his own mind as to what the child should know about Christ's death.
2. The teacher should be familiar enough with the Bible so as to help the child see for himself what the Bible teaches.
3. The teacher should repeat the truths of the salvation message over and over to children.
4. The teacher should be careful to explain the terms he uses.
5. The teacher should depend on the Holy Spirit.[9]

Of these basics listed by Miss Soderholm the latter is the most important. The Sunday school teacher must be led by the Holy Spirit in leading an unsaved child into the salvation experience. Since this is a spiritual rebirth the Holy Spirit is a very necessary Agent in the act. The trained teacher will soon be capable of determining when the fruit has ripened on the vine. The trained teacher will then assist the Holy Spirit in gathering the fruit.

THE PRESCHOOL CHILD
IN RETROSPECT

The Preschooler has ceased his rapid growth. He is going through a lengthening-out process but is not growing excessively. Instead he is now losing his "baby fat" and is leaner and harder. His demands for action are not lessened by this hardening process but increased. Because of the Preschooler's desire to be mobile the classroom must be of sufficient size to allow him to move about.

The Preschooler can do more than the Nursery child but he is still limited in what he can do. He does not have control of his finer muscles, therefore his activities must be limited to those things he can do. Nothing is more frustrating to the Preschooler than to be assigned tasks of which he is incapable.

The Preschooler's vocabulary has expanded by more than 1000 words by the time he reaches the age of 5 years and 6 months. The teacher must learn the vocabulary of the Preschooler and use that vocabulary in communicating with him. One of the best methods of learning the Preschooler's vocabulary is by observation, although there are several excellent books available that the teacher can use as a resource refuge.

The Preschooler is equipped with two valuable tools for learning—his curiosity and imagination. The Sunday school teacher must capture both of these tools if he expects to relate to his Preschoolers. Methods of teaching should be selected that arouse the curiosity and tease the imagination. Two excellent methods that the Preschool teacher may choose to use are storytelling and role playing.

The secret then that the Preschool teacher must learn is to discover where the Preschooler is, begin there, and build the child's learning experiences with the building blocks of knowledge. This new-found knowledge should pave the way for the child's conversion experience, if not now, then surely in his Primary and Junior years.

THE PRESCHOOL TEACHER

Every Preschool teacher should not only be a Christian, but also a growing Christian. This requirement is demanded of all Sunday school teachers for none can rightly divide the Word of Truth unless he knows the Author and is guided by Him.

The story is told of an atheist who greeted a child one Sunday morning with the question, "Where are you going so early?"

The freshly scrubbed, neatly dressed child answered, "I'm going to Sunday school."

The atheist raised his eyebrows and asked the child, "Why do you go to Sunday school?"

The child replied, "To learn about God."

"Harrumph, what makes you think there is a God?" continued the man.

The child answered without hesitation, " 'Cause my teacher knows Him."

There are other requirements demanded of the Preschool teacher as well as every other Sunday school teacher. They are:

1. Every teacher *must* be a member of the church in which he teaches.
2. Every teacher *must* have a good working knowledge of the 66 books of the Bible.
3. Every teacher *must* have a broad knowledge of Bible related subjects. These are such subjects as Bible geography, Bible history, and the life and customs of Bible times. The Preschool teacher will find some difficulty in breaking such knowledge down to the Preschool level but this does not lessen the requirement for such knowledge.
4. Every teacher *must* be acquainted with the techniques of teaching.
5. Every teacher *must* have a knowledge of Sunday school organization and administration.
6. Every teacher *must* know his pupils—in general and in particular.[10]

Perhaps one becomes overwhelmed at these demands that are made of Sunday school teachers. However, when one realizes that he is dealing with eternal souls the demands are not too great.

THE CLASSROOM SETTING

It is not a waste of money when a church builds

and furnishes a room for Preschoolers. These are impressionable years and an attractive place suitable for happy learning and worship experiences fosters in the children a love and respect for God's house.

The classroom should be located on the first floor of the educational building. Dimensional requirements were given earlier in this chapter. The walls of the classroom should be painted a light color. The classroom should be located near the restrooms and drinking fountain. The chairs in the classroom should be from 10 to 12 inches high. This allows the child to rest both feet firmly on the floor. The teacher should use one of these smaller chairs so she will not have to talk down to her pupils.

The room should be equipped with an adequate chalkboard and bulletin board. A piano or small organ will add to the musical program. Tables of the proper height will be needed. The floor should be covered with tile that is kept clean and sanitary. The teacher may choose to use a rug for the story-time center. Check the list of furnishings given in the previous chapter, for much of the material recommended for the Nursery child can also be used for the Preschooler.

CONCLUSION

The Preschool teacher cannot be a novice. The

better trained and most experienced teachers should serve on this level. One teacher is needed for every five to seven Preschoolers. Several teachers may work together until the enrollment exceeds the classroom capacity and then additional classroom space will be needed. Every segment of the program is designed for the child's spiritual edification. A good team of teachers can make the Sunday school hour meaningful and brief for the Preschooler who assumes that time passes ever so slowly when he is bored.

CHAPTER THREE

FOOTNOTES

[1] D. Bruce Gardner, *Development In Early Childhood* (New York, 1964), pp. 122–123.

[2] *Ibid.*, p. 131.

[3] Marjorie Elaine Soderholm, *Understanding the Pupil, Part I, The Preschool Child* (Grand Rapids, 1967), p. 40.

[4] Gardner, p. 176.

[5] John Milton Gregory, *The Seven Laws of Teaching* (Grand Rapids, 1965), pp. 51-53.

[6] Elizabeth B. Hurlock, *Child Development Fourth Edition* (New York, 1964), p. 506.

[7] *Ibid.*, pp. 338–339.

[8] Hazel N. Strickland and Mattie C. Leatherwood, *Beginner Sunday School Work* (Nashville, 1955), p. 5.

[9] Marjorie Elaine Soderholm, *Explaining Salvation to Children* (Minneapolis, 1962), pp. 10-11.

[10] Clarence H. Benson, *Teaching Techniques for Sunday School* (Wheaton, 1935), pp. 10-12.

CHAPTER THREE

QUESTIONS FOR REVIEW

1. How does a knowledge of the growth norms of a Preschooler help us in Sunday school?

2. Discuss the classroom dimensions and setting that are prescribed for Preschoolers.

3. Does the Preschooler have limited motor abilities?

4. How does the motor ability of the Preschooler affect his training in Sunday school?

5. Discuss the importance of the Law of the Language as well as the rules that regulate this law.

6. What are the two natural attributes of the Preschooler that can be used in the learning process? Discuss them.

7. Name two good methods suggested for use with Preschoolers.

8. Which is more important for the Preschooler, the kind or the number of social contacts he has? Discuss your answer.

9. Should every Preschool child be expected to experience the New Birth? Discuss your answer.

10. List the requirements for the Sunday school teacher.

CHAPTER FOUR

THE PRIMARY CHILD

Heretofore we have explored the characteristics of the children in their earlier stages of life in spans of two years each. The next several stages of the child's life will be approached in spans of three years each. The Primary child engulfs the ages of 6, 7 and 8. The name Primary is attached to this child because of the very meaning of the word—first in order in any series, sequence, etc. The Sunday school borrows the name from secular education, just as they borrowed the idea of the graded Sunday school. Since this is the stage where grading begins in the Sunday school it would be well if we pause parenthetically and look into this system of dividing Sunday school classes and departments.

THE GRADED SUNDAY SCHOOL

Group Grading. By placing the Primaries together in a group which includes all 6-7-8's we are involved in what is called group grading or department grading. Since the Bible is the basis of our study in the Sunday school this type of grading involves one's approach to Bible study. In department grading a different Bible content is provided for each department group. The Primaries will study portions of Scripture that are best suited for them while the Juniors, Intermediates, etc., will study those passages that are best suited for them. There are several advantages to this system of grading. First, all activities are closely related to the Bible lesson in each department group. Second, lessons can be geared to the social, psychological, emotional and mental level of all pupils. One pointed weakness of this system is that common at-home discussion is limited, since parents and children study different sections of the Bible.

Close Grading. When a Sunday school is closely graded the child is placed in the same grade that he occupies at the public school. It is assumed that this type of grading corresponds with the age of the child and thus should follow this pattern:

Age 6 — First Grade	Age 12 — Seventh Grade
Age 7 — Second Grade	Age 13 — Eighth Grade
Age 8 — Third Grade	Age 14 — Ninth Grade
Age 9 — Fourth Grade	Age 15 — Tenth Grade
Age 10 — Fifth Grade	Age 16 — Eleventh Grade
Age 11 — Sixth Grade	Age 17 — Twelfth Grade

The secular school has found that this type of grade placement is not without its problems. There is no provision made for the slow learner or the exceptional child. Some educators today are advocating a flexible system in which pupils can progress as freely as their growth and development will allow. Very little, if any, provision is made in the Sunday school hour to challenge the exceptionally bright child or to assist the slow learner. Perhaps we are justified in our complaint that "we just don't have sufficient time for specialties during the Sunday school hour."

In the closely graded Sunday school a different Bible content is provided for pupils in each public school grade. With this system, curriculum can be planned to fit the stage of development of pupils. Those who object to closely graded Sunday school literature do so on the basis that it too limits at-home discussion. Some also find it difficult to relate all of the activities in the Sunday school hour to the theme, since each grade has a different lesson.

Before we return to our original purpose let us give some more attention to grading. Either group grading or close grading is found to be valuable in Sunday school, especially as a growth incentive. One of the laws of Sunday school growth states that "the Sunday school can multiply by dividing." This calls for the continuous addition of new units—a unit can be a department or class. Grading by ages provides the most logical basis for adding new units. Note the following advantages of grading by ages:

1. Grading helps the teacher to meet the individual needs of the pupil.
2. Grading prevents the temptation to have teacher-centered classes.
3. Grading simplifies the teacher's task.

4. Grading puts more workers to work for Christ.
5. Grading paves the way for promotion which recognizes the natural laws of growth and progress.

THE PRIMARY CHILD'S GROWTH DEVELOPMENT

The Primary child enters the middle years of childhood at age six. The middle years continue until age 12 or puberty. These are rather tranquil years when they are compared to the turmoil of the preschool years and that of adolescence. The middle years begin with the loss of the first baby teeth and end at about the time the permanent teeth are all in, so that we can call this *the toothless age.* It will be quite common to have a Primary child greet you with a toothless grin on Sunday morning.

The Primary child remains in the period of slow growth that he entered at age two. His height and weight will increase slightly each year. This slow pace of growth allows the child to use his energy for play or work. From age two or three until puberty the normal, healthy child seems to have a boundless supply of energy. He wants to be on the go all the time and finds sitting still in Sunday school very difficult. He becomes restless if he cannot move around and do things during his waking hours, claiming that he is not tired, does not need a rest period during the day, or is "not sleepy" at bedtime. When free to play, he runs, climbs, and jumps constantly, shouting and laughing to let off extra energy. Although he is sometimes angry, cranky, or generally disagreeable, this is mainly because he feels that he has not been fairly treated, rarely because he is tired.[1]

We learned that the average five-year-old child will stand 3½ feet tall and weigh around 42 pounds. During the middle years the average child will grow approximately three inches annually with a weight gain of approximately ten pounds each year. The growth pattern will be the same for boys and girls during this period. The onset of puberty usually reaches girls before it does boys; therefore, the girls will normally outgrow the boys for a year or so. Once a boy enters puberty he too begins his second stage of rapid growth and in a very short time will stand head and shoulders above the girls. More discussion about puberty will follow in the next several chapters.

The Primary child's finer muscles are now beginning to develop. He can now handle the smaller crayons, color within the lines, and use scissors fairly well. He likes to do things and will enjoy workbooks and handcraft.

The Primary teacher can use the Primary child's ambition to "do things" as an instrument of teaching. Let us digress for the next several paragraphs to discuss

John Milton Gregory's *Law of the Learning Process.* The law of the learning process may be stated:

The pupil must reproduce in his own mind the truth to be learned.

This law presents the idea that teaching is pupil-centered and not teacher-centered. A teacher can demand that her pupils commit the lesson to memory, but this does not mean that the child understands what he has memorized or that he possesses the lesson. The child must be allowed to express himself about the subject matter he is being taught. When he is capable of doing this he understands what he has been taught. The real "proof of the pudding" in education comes in application. The child may be taught, "Be ye kind!", but an expression of kindness from his teacher and an act of kindness by himself will implant the lesson permanently.[2]

Years ago Marion Lawrence stated that "a child remembers 10% of what he hears, 50% of what he sees and 90% of what he does." This statement underscores the value of *expressional teaching aids*—those aids that allow the pupil to reproduce in expression the lesson he is learning. Workbooks and handcraft are valuable expressional teaching aids.

Many inexpensive materials are available for handcraft projects. These include construction paper, pasteboard, plastic, and plaster of Paris. Bible-times villages can be constructed from pasteboard, paper, wood, and cloth. Models of Bible-times homes, synagogues, and the Temple are available at most Christian bookstores. A class of Primaries can learn much more by constructing a model of the Tabernacle than they can by reading the Exodus "blueprint." Properly correlated activities will develop Christian character and Christian living.[3]

Hand Skills. By the time the child reaches age six he can model with clay, make cookies, sew, copy a diamond, and help with simple household tasks such as carrying glasses and pitchers of milk without spilling. After six years of age, skilled movements with the hands may be acquired quickly and easily if the child is given guidance and an opportunity to learn the most effective methods to use. Control of the fine muscles of the fingers develops at a slower rate as shown by the fact that the control necessary for speedy writing or the playing of musical instruments is not attained by most children until they are twelve years or older.[4]

THE PRIMARY CHILD'S
MENTAL DEVELOPMENT

The average Primary child has an IQ of 100. His IQ is established by his heredity and environment. It is determined by arriving at one's mental age through a series of tests. The mental age is then divided by the chronological age and multiplied by a hundred. The formula is written M.A./C.A. x 100. One's IQ (Intelligence Quotient) remains rather constant throughout one's lifetime.

As an average Primary, your Sunday school scholar has enrolled in the public school and has begun the training that has been standardized for every first-grader. The curriculum of the first-grader includes such items as learning to read and write. The three year span of 6 through 8 covers a wide variety of abilities among Primaries. The first grade child is just learning to recognize words while the third grade child has a much wider reading vocabulary. Hurlock lists the following writing skills of the Primary child:

6 years   Prints entire alphabet in large, irregular letters with many reversals. Copies words using all capitals with some reversal of letters and in the wrong order. Prints numbers 1-20, with frequent reversals in the numbers 3, 7, and 9.

7 years   Most children can write, though some still print in capitals. Writing is large, straight, labored, and irregular in size and shape. Numbers are smaller, but there are many errors.

8 years   Most children write by now, in large, square and quite black letters. Capitals and looped letters are disproportionately tall. Numbers are smaller, and there are fewer errors.[5]

The Primary child has a vocabulary of 2500 words when he enters the Primary Department and about 3600 words when he leaves. Perhaps the Primary age that will prove most difficult for the teacher is age six. The Primary child of this age is just beginning to learn how to read and write. A workbook for this six-year-old child will be of little value unless someone can help him with the answers. He will need help from someone in the use of his pupil's quarterly too. These problems will disappear as the Primary child reaches seven and eight or the second and third grades correspondingly.

The attention span of the Primary child is almost twice that of the Preschooler. He can give attention to something interesting for a span of seven to ten minutes. Marjorie Soderholm recommends that the Sunday school hour be divided into three twenty-minute periods in order to gain and hold the Primary child's attention. She writes:

Each of these periods should have some variation within it. The first period may be a worship-time with music, prayer, Scripture reading, and a feature such as a picture study, chalk talk, or projected slides. The second period may be the class-time for the Bible story and conversation about the application of the story to the lives of the boys and girls. The third period may be a time when the class plays the story or does some handwork related to the story. Sometimes a part of this period may be used for Bible drills and Bible games.[6]

The memory ability develops rapidly during the Primary years. The Primary child can now memorize verses of Scripture as well as their references. The verses may be shortened in length and should contain words that Primaries will understand.

The American Primary child lives in a fascinating era. Through the means of his television set he has witnessed men walking on the moon. His natural curiosity is aroused. He is fascinated by space travel, space exploration, and astronomy. He has come to ponder the mysteries of life, birth, and death. He has become aware of and is fascinated by the processes of his own body. Because he knows more he desires to know even more. The Primary Sunday school teacher can capture this active curiosity and utilize it for learning experiences. The Primary child loves questions. He likes both to ask questions and to be asked questions. The Primary teacher should be ready to answer the Primary child's questions. If the teacher does not know the answer he should be quick to admit it. The teacher should never try to bluff his way through an answer. Promise to furnish the answer in the future and then do it!

The Primary child has a good imagination. He has maintained his interest in animism. He is in the second stage of animistic concepts where consciousness is attributed only to things that move. The older Primary child will move into the third stage of animism and only attribute consciousness to those bodies that can move of their own accord. Storytelling (see the discussion about the story in the previous chapter) and role-playing are two effective methods to use with Primaries.

The Primary child is literal-minded. He has some ability to reason but the abstract is still beyond his understanding. He may not grasp the meaning of an object lesson or a song. One Primary child returned from Sunday school and said they sang about a bear. The parents and teacher were puzzled because no song about a bear was sung. Then they discovered the stanza, "Gladly, the Cross I'd Bear" was misinterpreted to be "Gladly, the Cross-eyed Bear." Another Primary child was asked to draw a Bible picture and proudly presented an airplane with four people aboard. When asked to describe the drawing he said that it represented the "flight" into Egypt. The three people in the back seat of the plane were Mary, Joseph and Baby Jesus. "Who is that seated in the front seat?" "Why its Pontius the Pilot, of course!"

THE PRIMARY CHILD'S
SOCIAL DEVELOPMENT

Upon entering school the child enters the "gang age"—an age when social consciousness develops rapidly and when becoming socialized is one of the major developmental tasks. The childhood gang is not necessarily composed of "hoodlums," though children's gangs in slum areas often are made up of children who are regarded as such by society. The typical child's gang is a *play group*, made up of children who have common play interests.[7]

The six-year-old is likely to be but a fringe member of the gang. He will imitate their ways and do the bidding of older children, but his allegiance is still pledged to adults. By the time he reaches eight he will be a full-fledged member of the gang and completely "weaned away" from his reliance upon adult circles. He becomes a member of the peer group and this group will gradually replace the family in its influence over his behavior and attitudes. The peer group is an "aggregation of people of approximately the same age who feel and act together"—Hurlock. This gang spirit does not necessarily die out with childhood but may extend well into adulthood. Adults unite with fraternal organizations, lodges, and clubs and live under rules and rituals.

The gang begins to dominate the child's life. It sets the style in the clothing he wants to wear, determines the play activities he engages in, and gives him his ideas of right and wrong. Gangs develop their own system of rules and regulations (whether adopted or unadopted). When a child belongs to a gang it gives him companionship, an opportunity to have fun, and a feeling of pride and status. Boys, as a rule, start to form gangs earlier than girls. Both lose interest in gang life at puberty.

Games That Children Play. The Primary child is exposed to Little League Baseball, and Pee Wee Football. Psychologists are still exploring the effects of thrusting children into this type of early competitive activity. The common games are still participated in by every generation. Children still play hide-and-seek, tag, hopscotch, blindman's buff, Red Rover, dodge-ball, jacks, London Bridge, ring-around-a-rosy, jump rope, etc., as they have for centuries. These are all group or gang games. Many of the games have accompanying chants. You may hear some of them around Sunday school. Have you ever heard, "Last one in is a rotten egg," "I scream, you scream, we all scream for ice cream," "It's raining, it's pouring, my daddy's inside a snoring," "No more spelling, no more books, no more teacher's dirty looks," "School's out, school's out, The teacher let the monkeys out," "Rain, rain, go away, come back some other day," "Susie's mad, and I'm glad, and I know how to please her"? Of course you are familiar with these chants. You said them when you were small. The children did not learn them from you, they learned them from their own small society.

The Primary Sunday school teacher must be aware of the fact that these are crucial years for the Primary child. These are years of social adjustment. Primary boys are not interested in Primary girls and it may be best to house them in separate classrooms. Group activities can be planned. Every child must be included in the group activities. Every child must be given the sense of belonging. Your Primaries will begin to pair off and find best buddies. This is not objectionable but natural.

The Primary child has a strong sense of justice. At the beginning of the Sunday school year you might seek his assistance in compiling a list of do's and don't's for the class. Let the class determine what should become of the disobedient. You may be surprised to discover that the standards set by the class will be higher than those you would have imposed. Keep in mind that your Primaries are "doers." They want to be involved so why not involve them?

THE PRIMARY CHILD'S
SPIRITUAL DEVELOPMENT

We have learned that the Primary child is becoming gregarious. He likes going to Sunday school because of the opportunity it affords him of being with his peers. He likes Sunday school because it affords him an opportunity of self-expression. He likes Sunday school because of the Bible stories that are told.

The Primary child may be ready to accept Christ as his Savior. Evelyn Nown, a children's specialist, has stated an urgent truth, "Perhaps parents and teachers would work with new zeal and vision if they stopped to realize that the film of childhood can never be run through for a second showing."[8] Your Primaries are only going to pass through this stage of life once. If they are not reached for Christ today you may not be able to reach them tomorrow. An anonymous poet has written the following truthful poem titled "The Plastic Years."

They pass so quickly, the days of youth
  And the children change so fast,
And soon they harden in the mould,
  And the plastic years are past.

Then shape their lives while they are young,
  This be our prayer, our aim,
That every child we meet, shall bear
  The imprint of His name.

The Primary child is not ready to accept deep theological concepts nor is he worried about denominational beliefs. He can accept the cardinal truths of the Bible. He will accept the fact that the Bible was written by God and that every word of it is true. Inspiration and revelation mean nothing to the Primary. It is best he remember that the Bible is God's Book and contains the message that God wants us to have. The Primary child conceives of God as a person, made of flesh and blood. God can see everything, everywhere and He spends His time watching people to see how they behave. Most children think of God's abode as in the heavens or in the clouds. They believe in miracles and accept the fact that God can do anything. How tragic it is that some Primaries pass through the Junior and Intermediate ages and lose their childhood faith in the Bible and in God.[9]

The Primary child does have a concept of sin and sin bothers him. He can understand that Jesus died on the cross to save him from his sins. Some Primaries are ready to accept Christ but the teacher is incapable of leading them to Christ. In the previous chapter there were six *"musts"* that are demanded of every teacher. It is time now to list the seventh and most important. *Every Sunday school teacher must be able to lead his unsaved pupils to Christ.* It is tragic that some teachers recognize the ripening of the fruit on the vine but have to sound the alarm for the Pastor or someone else in the church to come and pick the fruit. It is easy to lead the prepared heart to the Savior; it is only the getting at it that is difficult. Someone has said that salvation is as simple as A, B, C. This statement can be worked into the following formula for soulwinning:

A—*Ask*
Romans 10:13 "For whosoever shall call upon the name of the Lord *shall be saved.*"

B—*Believe*
Acts 16:31 "Believe on the Lord Jesus Christ, and thou *shalt be saved . . . .*"

C—*Confess*
Romans 10:9 "That if thou shalt confess with thy mouth the Lord Jesus, and shalt believe in thine heart that God hath raised him from the dead, thou *shalt be saved.*"

Each of these verses deals with the definiteness of salvation as they each use the strong language of, "*Thou shalt be saved.*"

The Primary child can begin to develop a working acquaintance with the Bible. He should be encouraged to bring his Bible to Sunday school. He must come to understand that the Bible is the basic textbook of the Sunday school and he would not think of going to school without his textbooks. Your pupils can begin to learn the locations of the various books of the Bible as well as some of the important verses of the Bible.

You should encourage your Primary children to develop their own devotional lives. If they are from Christian homes they have already been introduced to "grace" at the table and bed-time devotionals. Each child should be taught the value of private prayer. Each child should be encouraged to participate in and lead public prayer. The latter may be more difficult. The timid child may not wish to lead a public prayer and should not be forced or coaxed to do so. Through proper encouragement this bashful boy or girl can be led into this action.

The Primary child should be encouraged to become a good steward. Your pupils probably perform some chores for which they receive some allowance. It is not too early to encourage them to tithe their allowance. Small gifts to missions can be encouraged. The giver of pennies in childhood can become the giver of dollars in adulthood.

The Primary child will like to participate in the worship program of the Sunday school. He loves to sing and will especially enjoy participating in action choruses. He likes Bible memory verses and he should be encouraged to use them in worship services.

Children's Church. Should the Primary child attend the morning worship service? Of course he should unless some provision is made to have special services for the children. These special services are called *Children's Church.* More will be said about this ministry several paragraphs removed from this one.

Your Primary class should learn the various functions of the church building—the purpose of the pulpit, the organ, the stained-glass windows, the Communion Table, the Baptistry and other various aspects of the church.

Your Primaries must learn to reverence the church building. This can be learned from example. Someone has said that "order is as contagious as disorder." An orderly program, an orderly atmosphere, an orderly arrangement of things is sure to produce a deep feeling of respect. Order must be preceded by promptness. All of the services at church should have an announced starting time and start at that time. Primary years are impressionable years. The Primary child imitates the doer rather than the deed.

Some churches have sufficient space to house a Children's Church. Children's Church can be graded according to departments or grouped by combining several departments. Children's Church is not a second Sunday school hour. Quarterlies, workbooks, and handcraft are all laid aside after the Sunday school hour and the children come together to worship. This hour is not just something else to do nor is it a baby-sitting service. It is a worship service that is geared to the children's level.

Every phase of the program is designed with the children in mind. The children can participate in the service.

An assembly room is needed that is large enough to house a pulpit, chairs (placed in neat rows) and piano or organ. The Children's Church will need a director as well as assistants. Here is a suggested program for the service.

*Call to worship
 Prayer
 Welcome to Visitors
 Offering
 Offering Prayer
*Doxology
 Song Time
 Bible Story
*Choruses
 Missionary Emphasis
*Chorus and Stretch Time
 Conduct Story
*Closing Song (Invitation)
*Prayer   (*Stand)

You can see that the program is not unlike that of the Adult Worship Hour. The difference is that the children participate in worship with those nearer their own age level and are involved in a program that is designed with them in mind.

THE PRIMARY CHILD
IN RETROSPECT

The Primary child has turned six and started to the first grade at the public school. If he attends a Sunday school that is closely graded he also is placed in a first grade class. If his Sunday school is not closely graded then he is placed in the same room with seven- and eight-year-old children.

Your Primary student may greet you with a toothless grin. He has begun to shed his baby teeth and grow his permanent ones. His growth rate is slow and almost unnoticed during his three years in the Primary department. He will grow less than one foot during this period. His slow growth gives him an overabundance of energy. This burst of energy and vitality can be directed towards learning experiences as one of the best ways of learning is by doing.

The launching of the Primary child's educational experience opens avenues of new learning for him as he learns to read and write during the first several grades at school. This, of course, benefits the Sunday school teacher as new doors of teaching are opened to him. The Primary child also learns to utilize his memory. The Primary teacher will exercise but not overtax this ability to memorize by suggesting abbreviated verses of Scripture.

The Primary child begins to turn away from the adult world to a world of his peers. The Primary teacher must be aware of this socialization of the Primary and take advantage of it. The Sunday school hour provides an opportunity for the child to be with his peers. The Primary teacher must provide an opportunity for the child to learn alongside his peers and not apart from them.

The Primary child is concerned about spiritual matters and may be ready to receive Christ as his Savior. The Primary teacher *must* be prepared to lead his unsaved pupils to Christ. It is his responsibility; he should not expect someone else to carry out this responsibility for him.

THE PRIMARY TEACHER

The Primary teacher must have a winsome personality. Winning the child to himself is the first step in winning him to Christ. The Primary teacher (and every Sunday school teacher) must have a definite purpose in teaching. That purpose is to take every pupil's hand and lead him directly to the Savior.

The Primary teacher must have a definite reason for teaching. The ministry of teaching is a holy calling. It carries the same Biblical foundation as preaching. The Primary teacher is involved in the Great Commission. You are acquainted with the following verses:

Matthew 28:19-20

Go ye therefore, and teach all nations, baptizing them in the name of the Father, and of the Son, and of the Holy Ghost:

Teaching them to observe all things whatsoever I have commanded you: and, lo, I am with you alway, even unto the end of the world. Amen.

The first words in each of these two verses spell out the greatest command in the Great Commission—"*Go . . . Teaching!*" An important and timely question is "Why are you teaching?" Are you teaching to please the Sunday school Superintendent? Are you teaching because you were elected to the position? Are you teaching because you feel a strong sense of duty? Your answer to these questions should be a loud, firm "No!" You *must* teach because God has called you to teach.

THE CLASSROOM SETTING

The Primary classroom should be one of the lightest, brightest, cheeriest and best equipped rooms. It should be a room that is kept at the right temperature the year around. The room should have adequate lighting, clean curtains, painted furniture, beautiful colored pictures and tasteful decorations. Special low tables suited to the size of the children are an important asset. There should be an adequate supply of chairs, adjusted to the height of the children.

Each room should be equipped with a chalkboard, bulletin board, cabinet, coat rack, and flags. (Your Primary children should be taught to salute the flags and the Bible.) A vase of flowers will brighten and freshen the room. The room should be kept uncluttered and clean. A small piano or organ will be an asset to your total teaching program. If it is not possible to tile the floor, then paint it and wax it once the paint is dry.

CONCLUSION

The Primary teacher is called of God to the teaching task. He then enters a training program to prepare for the task. This book is designed as an aid in this preparation. Once the teacher is trained he is ready to begin the tremendous undertaking of teaching the Bible and leading his pupils to Christ. Sunday school teaching is a challenging call to service and rewarding experiences.

CHAPTER FOUR

FOOTNOTES

[1] Elizabeth B. Hurlock, *Child Development Fourth Edition* (New York, 1956), p. 18.

[2] Clarence H. Benson, *Teaching Techniques for Sunday School* (Wheaton, 1935), pp. 28-29.

[3] *Ibid.*, pp. 38-39.

[4] Hurlock, p. 192.

[5] Hurlock, p. 194.

[6] Marjorie Elaine Soderholm, *Understanding the Pupil, Part II, The Primary and Junior Child* (Grand Rapids, 1961), pp. 15-16.

[7] Hurlock, pp. 354-355.

[8] Clyde M. Narramore, *How to Understand and Influence Children* (Grand Rapids, 1957), p. 65.

[9] Hurlock, p. 602.

CHAPTER FOUR

QUESTIONS FOR REVIEW

1. How does the Primary child become involved in the graded Sunday school?

2. Discuss the two different methods of grading.

3. How can the Primary teacher best direct the Primary child's boundless energy?

4. What problem must the Primary teacher who teaches six-year-olds cope with that the teacher of sevens and eights does not face?

5. Discuss the social implications of the Primary child.

6. Can a Primary child be won to Christ? If so, how?

7. What can the Primary child understand about the Bible? What can he not understand?

8. How can the Primary child be encouraged in worship?

9. Write your own summary to this chapter.

10. Why must the Primary teacher be called of God to the teaching task?

CHAPTER FIVE

THE JUNIOR CHILD

Blair and Burton, collaborators in writing the book *Growth and Development of the Preadolescent*, rightly conclude that "the literature in elementary education and in child psychology shows clearly that the age roughly from nine until puberty is the forgotten period of childhood."[1] Volumes have been written about infancy and the early childhood periods. Libraries are filled with books about adolescents. The secular writer has had little to say about the preadolescent or the later years of childhood. The sacred writer has focused on this age level for one basic reason—this is usually the age of conversion. If the child is not converted as a Beginner or Primary then surely he will be converted during his Junior years. If he is not converted during his Junior years he may never be reached for Christ. More decisions are made for Christ during the Junior age (9-11) than at any other time.

The name given to the preadolescent by the Sunday school is Junior. No one is quite sure of the origin of this title that is assigned to ages 9-11. The dictionary does indicate that the use of this title is peculiar to the Sunday school. The ages of 9-11 will normally correspond with grades four, five, and six in secular education. Grading of the Sunday school was discussed in the previous chapter.

THE PHYSICAL GROWTH
OF THE JUNIOR

The yearly growth increments for the Junior child are the least of all growth periods until maturity. During these years of 9-11 physical and organic growth is stable. It is as though nature is storing up growth nutrients for the next period of maturation.

Since the Junior child does not direct his energy towards growth he must channel it in other directions. Juniors can play strenuous games longer, run faster, throw and catch much better, and climb and jump with great ease and assurance. His outstanding physical developments are (1) increased manual dexterity, (2) increased strength, and (3) increased resistance to fatigue. [2]

Motor Development. There is little the Junior child cannot do and little he will not want to do. His increased muscular and motor coordination has opened new doors to the Junior. Exercise is now a norm rather than the exception. This abundance of exercise will make the Junior years the healthiest of his lifetime. The Junior has already experienced many of the childhood diseases.

The continuing development of motor skills is important to the Junior child. Good motor control will contribute to good mental health. Strenuous play frees the child from the tensions of anxiety and frustration.

Motor control will also contribute to the Junior child's socialization. He can now do many more things with his peers whose skills are similar to his. He will be pleased with any opportunity afforded him to illustrate that his skills are even better than his peers.

Good motor activity helps to build the child's *self-concept.* The child who successfully develops good motor skills also develops physical security. Physical security is soon translated into psychological security. This acquirement of self-confidence also leads to the child's independence. The more he can do for himself the greater his self-confidence and happiness will be.

Puberty. There are many misconceptions about puberty. This is illustrated by the fact that, in law, twelve is commonly designated as the age for girls and fourteen for boys. The concept of an age of accountability in theological circles is probably associated with puberty.

The word puberty comes from the Latin word *pubertos,* meaning "age of manhood." The transition from child to adult does not take place instantly. On the average, puberty spans from 2 to 4 years.[3] Normally the Junior boy does not enter puberty, as this stage of development is reserved for his next age level. The Junior girl may enter the early stages of puberty at age 11. This subject is only introduced here; it will be discussed in greater detail in the next chapter. Suffice it to say now that these dormant years of growth will be followed by major physiological changes that will occur during the early years of adolescence.

Appearance. One nine-year-old boy remarked, "Time sure passes quick. Today is Wednesday. It's only been three days since I've had my bath and in three days I'll have to take another one."

The Junior has no problem in caring for his own physical needs and appearance. He simply doesn't have the time to bother with them. He may spend time before the mirror combing his hair and then run out to play and never give his hair another thought. He can be dressed neatly one moment and have ruffled clothes and his shirt-tail hanging out the next. It is common for him to kick a ball and scuff his new shoes. The following recipe for a soiled Junior has been prepared:

Take:
    1 large grassy field
    ½ dozen children
    2 or 3 small dogs
    a pinch of brook and pebbles

Mix children and dogs well and put them in a field, stirring constantly. Pour brook over pebbles; sprinkle field with flowers; spread over a deep blue sky and bake in the sun. When thoroughly brown, remove clothing for the washer and place children in tub of warm water with lots of soap suds.

THE MENTAL GROWTH
OF THE JUNIOR

As children grow older the majority of them improve in their ability to do more complicated intellectual tasks. A few reliable studies report that the child's capacity for more accurate thinking is developed in those years that precede adolescence. The child of 9-11 transfers from fantasy to reality in his thought life. The Junior child will also experience growth in the use of his reading skills.

The World of Words. The average desk dictionary will contain 140,000 words. No one knows the exact number of words in the English vocabulary. It contains at least 600,000 words. Language is always in a constant change. New words are being introduced and old words are dying. When a language ceases to change it ceases to exist.

Everyone has two vocabularies—his active or use vocabulary which consists of words used in speaking or writing and his passive or recognition vocabulary which consists of words that are understood when listening or reading. A person's recognition vocabulary is usually many times larger than his use vocabulary. The average American adult may have a use vocabulary of 10,000 words but a recognition vocabulary of 30,000 or 40,000 words.[4]

Everyone should attempt to broaden his

vocabulary. The range of one's vocabulary is a clue to one's culture, education and general intelligence.

Vocabulary scales have been given in previous chapters but now one is no longer necessary. The Junior child will have a vocabulary of nearly 4,000 words and he will expand his word knowledge rapidly through the process of education. By the time he completes college he should have access to some 30,000 words.

What good are words? Someone has said that "words are the vehicles upon which thoughts ride." Words are a means of self-expression and communication. K. C. Garrison, author of *Growth and Development*, has said, "The number of words a child learns determines in large measure his school progress, and failure to progress normally has far reaching significance."

The Junior child is ready to receive and understand some theological terminology. Juniors are constantly seeking for the truth. They are ready to accept the fact that the Bible is God's Word. They will accept and believe the Biblical account of creation. They believe in keeping the rules. They can understand that we have broken the rules and that God's Son died on the cross to pay the penalty for our breaking the rules. The great cardinal doctrines of the Bible can find a home in the belief center of the Junior.

The World of Books. The Junior child loves to read. He will read everything he sees in writing from cereal boxes to road signs. If he doesn't understand a word he will ask its meaning. He will rapidly devour many of the books at the lending library. He can be encouraged to go through many of the books at the church library. He loves adventure and will enjoy reading the many missionary biographies that are available. The Junior child should be instructed to read his Bible daily and to prepare his Sunday school lesson each week. Television is competing for the Junior's mind and time. He will never learn as much from the TV set as he will from the world of books.

The World of Memory. The Junior age is often called the golden age of memory. Children memorize by employing two methods:

1. Repetition.

This is the centuries old method of learning by rote. When education is regarded as the acquisition of knowledge then repetition is used. The child repeats the information over and over under the guidance of a tutor until he can repeat the information mechanically.

2. Association.

Here the law of apperception is applied to memory. The law of apperception is that mental process through which new conceptions are interpreted in terms of the old.[5]

John Milton Gregory calls the law of apperception the Law of the Lesson: *The truth to be taught must be learned through truth already known.* Gregory suggests some simple rules to achieve success with this law:

1. Start where your pupils are.
2. Relate each new lesson to former lessons.
3. Arrange your presentation in natural steps.
4. Proportion the size of the steps to the ages and abilities of your pupils.
5. Use familiar illustrations.
6. Let your pupils find illustrations.
7. Let your pupils make use of their own knowledge.[6]

THE SOCIAL GROWTH OF THE JUNIOR

The 9-11 child faces two worlds socially. One is the world of adults and the other is the world of other children. Each group influences the Junior child and helps to shape his world.

The World of Children. We have learned that a child is introduced to the "gang" when he begins public school. During his Junior years the child is more active in the gang than at any other time of his life. At puberty he tends to lose interest in the gang and become attracted to the opposite sex.

The Junior child must have his basic needs met. These are the needs of food, physical comfort, love, and approval. The needs for food and physical comfort are readily met and the average Junior gives little thought to them. The basic needs of love and approval may also be met at home but the Junior child will seek to satisfy these needs with his peers. If he is successful he gains confidence in himself as an individual. If he fails to receive the approval of his peers a failure concept can be formed that may haunt him during his entire life span.

The Primary child often imitates his teacher and wants his approval. The preadolescent or Junior child shows more interest in group activity and is deeply loyal to that group. The approval of the teacher is unimportant in comparison with that of the gang.

Various studies have been completed that delve into the mysteries of the "gang age." Some of the results are as follows:

1. The gangs tend to reject adult leadership. Organized programs or play groups are usually not successful below age twelve. When adults attempt to direct the programs or groups they disintegrate. Play groups that spring up among children of the same age generally meet the ordinary needs of children below twelve.

2. During the Junior years the interest in the

organization itself rather than the activity of the organization is greater. Clubs with passwords, initiations, and an attitude of exclusiveness of "you can't belong" become frequent. "The Dirty Dozen," "The Three Musketeers," "Jones Street Gang" are some typical names. The clubs sometimes take on unique forms.

3. Most of the groups are small in number. They usually consist of not less than four or more than eight members. The motivation is a drive for individual status. Ties are formed on the basic common attitude towards authority. Leadership may only exist to the extent that leaders are chosen.[7]

Boys and girls of the Junior age level do not share the same interests or enjoy the same games. Girls and boys organize in different ways and for different reasons. Girls organize for social activity while boys organize for physical activity. There is a definite cleavage between the two sexes during the 9-11 years. Boys and girls belittle one another's interests, skills and activities; they refuse to associate with one another even at parties; and they are constantly bickering, name calling and quarreling.

There are several advantages that the child gains from the gang life. It teaches him to be democratic, to fit his desires and actions to those of the group, to cooperate with the group, to develop skills which will enable him to do what his peers do, and to eliminate selfishness and individualism.

There are also disadvantages derived from the gang life. Such undesirable qualities as swearing and use of slang are developed. Mischievousness and delinquency are the results of grouping together to seek and explore those areas that are considered to be off limits. Gang life can lead to the breakdown of ideals established in the home. It is fortunate that most children eliminate many of the undesirable habits they learn from the gang as they grow older.[8]

The World of Adults. The Sunday school teacher can wield an influence over Juniors but such influence can best be wielded by example. It will not take a Junior very long to spot a phony. The Junior teacher must walk his talk.

The Sunday school teacher cannot ignore the gang and its influence over boys and girls. The wise teacher will seek to guide the group in the proper direction. Such influence must be accomplished tactfully since adult leadership is generally rejected. The Junior will enjoy his Sunday school class if it is a club in which he can have an active part. The teacher must be a member of the club rather than the "dictator" of it.

Because of the cleavage that exists between the two sexes it is best to separate the Junior boys from the Junior girls during the Sunday school hour. An athletic minded male who is dedicated to the Lord and to his task would make a good teacher for the Junior boys. He can participate in the many outdoor activities that Junior boys enjoy. Since girl groups prefer socialization as their prime mover a woman who is as equally dedicated as her male counterpart would make a better teacher for the Junior girls.

THE SPIRITUAL GROWTH
OF THE JUNIOR

It has already been pointed out that the Junior age is the age of conversion. It should become a point of vital concern if a child is permitted to pass on to the Junior High department without recording a decision for Christ. The greatest failure of the Sunday school is the inability to hold on to its scholars after they finish the childhood days. Sixty-five percent of the girls and seventy percent of the boys drift away to become the religious derelicts of the community. Only a small percentage of them are brought back to the church through the efforts of revival and personal soul-winning.

Decisions for Christ in childhood prepare the way for other important decisions in adolescence. A decision for Christ in childhood will help to inspire the adolescent to prolong his educational period. It will also prepare the heart for the decision relative to Christian service while there is still time and opportunity for adequate preparation.[9]

The Age of Hero Worship. The Junior age is the age of hero worship. Boys tend to find their heroes in everyday life while girls are more likely to obtain their heroes from books. What boy has not idolized some star pitcher or prominent quarterback? Most boys can quote the vital statistics of their idol. They know how many games have been won and lost. They know his earned-run average. They know the total number of pass completions and number of yards gained.

The Sunday school teacher can direct this hero worship towards the Bible. The Bible is a hall of fame of heroes. The boys will become excited over the stories of Joseph, David, and Daniel. The girls will like the stories of Esther and Ruth.

Dr. Clarence Benson makes an important point about hero worship.

> As all Roman roads lead to the imperial city, so all Bible ideals should lead to Christ. Jesus is the Hero of heroes. The culmination of all hero lessons will be to bring the children to find their ideal in Christ. As the Old Testament characters are in so many instances types of the coming Messiah, so all hero lessons should be stepping stones to the Hero of all heaven and earth.[10]

A Time for Bible Study. Once a child is won to

Christ he must be won to God's Word. Every Junior should have a copy of the Bible for his very own. Educators say that the Junior's Bible should be printed in at least 11 point type. The Sunday school quarterly should never be substituted for the Bible. The teacher should teach directly from the Bible, and the pupil should have his Bible open.

There are certain facts that the Junior should know about the Bible. He can learn the books of the Bible in their order. This basic knowledge will help him immensely throughout all the years of his Bible study. The Junior student can learn something of the geography of Bible lands. A good set of Bible maps ought to be standard equipment for each classroom. Juniors will enjoy locating and pointing out places of vital interest pertinent to the immediate lesson. A knowledge of the customs of Bible days will help the Junior to understand the Bible. If he does not learn these customs then his study of the Bible can become confusing.

There are certain truths the Junior is ready to accept about the Bible. He can understand that the Bible is the inspired Word of God. The teacher can list the many human authors who were used in writing God's Book but also show that in reality there was only one Author and that was God's Holy Spirit (2 Timothy 3:16).

The Junior can be made aware of the fact that the Bible has a message for him. The same Holy Spirit who guided those who wrote the Bible, helps Juniors to understand the Bible and its message. The Junior needs to know that God expects him to obey the teachings of the Bible and that the Bible is the final authority in all matters.

An Introduction to Missions. The Junior has heard about missionaries before reaching the Junior age. His prior knowledge has come through the missionary stories he was told as a Preschooler and Primary. Now he can broaden his knowledge of missions. He must come to realize that the whole world is the mission field and that every Christian can be a missionary. The Junior can pray for the missionaries as well as contribute towards their support.

THE JUNIOR CHILD
IN RETROSPECT

One of the most important age levels of the Sunday school is the Junior level. This level is probably the most demanding and requires trained, dedicated teachers. If the Junior child passes through this department without being won to Christ the chances are good that he will never be won to Christ.

The Junior child is a doer. He hurries everywhere he goes even though he may not be going anywhere. He is always climbing, jumping, running, and wrestling. This excessive energy will cause the Junior teacher to face many problems unless he learns how to harness that energy and put it to useful projects. The Junior child cares little about his appearance and will readily discard his necktie and suitcoat. He is not bothered if his shirt-tail hangs out.

The Junior child has broadened his vocabulary considerably as he has progressed through the school grades. He will need assistance with theological terms and geographical locations but he can soon master words like these as he has supercalifragilisticexpialidocious.

Ages 9-11 can be called the age of books. The Junior will read more books average wise than he will read in any three-year period during the following years of his life. This age level is the appropriate age to encourage daily Bible reading. The Junior's appetite for reading can be directed to his Sunday school quarterly as well as the many good books that can be found in the church library.

The Junior Sunday school scholar has an active memory. He can learn the books of the Bible in their proper order as well as many verses of Scripture. Bible memory verse packets are available that will assist in Bible memorization. Juniors will enjoy participating in Bible drills and Bible games.

The Junior child is gregarious. He would rather associate with his peers than with adults. Junior boys will not want to associate with Junior girls. Problems are created when the boys and girls are grouped together in the same class.

THE JUNIOR TEACHER

The Junior teacher should review the requirements that are listed for the Preschool and Primary teacher. All Sunday school teachers must be examples. They must be able to say more than "Do as I teach." They must be the example that says "Do as I do." The Junior teacher must live so that his life says, "Follow me as I follow Christ."

One virtue that the Junior teacher needs is that of patience. The teacher who is constantly saying in a cross tone of voice, "Johnny, don't do that!" will find it difficult to convince his class of his love for them. Discipline will be a problem that must be dealt with firmly but one can be firm and kind at the same time. The best method to achieve good discipline in the classroom is for the teacher to be the master of his subject. The lesson that has been well prepared will make a strong contribution to an orderly classroom.

THE CLASSROOM SETTING

Dr. Clarence Benson points out three D's to be

watchful for in relationship to the classroom setting.

1. Watch for *discomforts*. Many classrooms have poor ventilation. Some contain space heaters with little or no ventilation. These space heaters compete for the air Juniors must breathe while they are in the classroom. It does not take long for an oxygen shortage to develop and the classroom to become uncomfortable. Care should be made to see that each classroom has some form of temperature control as well as proper ventilation.

2. Watch for *distractions*. The best way to limit outside distractions is for each class to have its own classroom. There are many ways to prevent visual distractions but one must watch for audio distractions as well.

3. Watch for *disturbances*. Secretaries and superintendents need to avoid disturbing Sunday school classes. Records must be kept and offerings taken but this *must* be done with as little disturbance as possible. The teacher has a limited time in which to present his lesson. His task is always made more difficult when there are continuous disturbances.[11]

The Junior-age children may be ready for regular, adult-size chairs but there are chairs available which are considered to be Junior size. The teacher will find that the children can work best at a table. When the class is seated at a table then the teacher will find it quite natural to be seated as he teaches.

A musical instrument and Junior hymnals are necessary equipment to help set the proper mood for the lesson. Juniors enjoy singing and they are ready to sing some of the simple hymns and choruses. Junior hymnals are available from your Christian bookstore.

The standard equipment such as chalkboard, bulletin board, and the Christian and American flags ought to appear in every classroom. Classroom walls can be decorated with posters and pictures. Juniors will enjoy sharing in the decorating of the classroom. They need to be taught to take pride in their classroom. In teaching them this lesson we will be teaching them an even greater one—to show respect and reverence for God's house.

CONCLUSION

The Junior teacher must make an all-out effort to win his pupils to Christ. Once this has been accomplished then the teacher must begin the work of follow-up training. The great task of Christian education is threefold—to bring the pupil to Christ, to train him up in Christ, and to send him out for Christ.

CHAPTER FIVE

FOOTNOTES

[1]Arthur Witt Blair and William H. Burton, *Growth and Development of the Preadolescent* (New York, 1951), p. 5.

[2]*Ibid.*, p. 139.

[3]Elizabeth B. Hurlock, *Child Development* (New York, 1964), p. 136.

[4]"Vocabulary," *The World Book Encyclopedia*, 1969 XIX, p. 337.

[5]Clarence H. Benson, *An Introduction to Child Study* (Chicago, 1945), pp. 154-155.

[6]John Milton Gregory, *The Seven Laws of Teaching* (Grand Rapids, 1965), pp. 57-70.

[7]Blair and Burton, pp. 45-47.

[8]Hurlock, pp. 368-369.

[9]Benson, pp. 167-168.

[10]*Ibid.*, p. 160.

[11]Clarence H. Benson, *Teaching Techniques for Sunday School* (Wheaton, 1935), p. 73.

CHAPTER FIVE

QUESTIONS FOR REVIEW

1. List the ages of the Junior as well as the corresponding grades for the graded Sunday school.

2. Why is the Junior age level one of the most important age levels in the Sunday school?

3. How can the Junior teacher best direct the Junior child's excessive energy?

4. How can the Junior teacher help to satisfy the Junior child's appetite for reading?

5. How can the Junior teacher best utilize the Junior child's capacity for memorization?

6. Who influences the Junior child's life the most? His peers? Adults? Discuss your answer.

7. How can the Junior teacher direct the Junior pupil's idolization of heroes toward Bible study?

8. Why is the Junior teacher's life example so important?

9. List the three D's that one must be watchful for in the classroom setting. How well do these three D's describe your Sunday school classroom?

10. Draw a standard size classroom for Juniors and place the essential equipment within the room.

THE JUNIOR HIGH YOUTH

It seems that everyone is interested in the adolescent. This is evident in the prodigious amount of recent literature dealing with adolescence. Systematic studies, controlled observation, and experimental research have eliminated some of the earlier misconceptions of adolescent development.

Adolescence is derived from a Latin verb *adolescere* meaning "to grow up" or "to grow into maturity." Dr. Rolf E. Muuss lists the following general definitions of adolescence:

> Sociologically, adolescence is the transition period from dependent childhood to self-sufficient adulthood. Psychologically, it is a "marginal situation" in which new adjustments have to be made, namely those that distinguish child behavior from adult behavior in a given society. Chronologically, it is the time span from approximately twelve or thirteen to the early twenties. It tends to occur earlier in girls than in boys.[1]

Adolescence begins with the introduction of puberty. This subject was introduced in the previous chapter. The main idea in the definition of puberty is the attainment of reproductive maturity. Puberty will normally cover a period of four years. At the end of this time period the child has been transformed to an adult.

The transition is only physical. Emotionally and mentally, the child is not ready to enter the adult world. The transition in these areas takes place in the later years of adolescence.

The Junior High student is at the threshold of adolescence and in the midst of puberty. He is leaving his childhood behind and approaching adulthood. In a sense he is neither a child nor an adult. Because he is in a stage of transition the Junior High student will find it difficult to identify himself.

THE CHANGING BODY

Parents will remember the difficulty they had in keeping their children in the proper-sized clothing when they were babies. The difficulty is more pronounced during the early years of adolescence. Long arms and legs just do not fit the standard sizes of clothes.

A New Body. The exterior changes of the body during early adolescence are often so radical that the adolescent may not be recognized at first glance by those who have not seen him for a period of time. The changes that take place within the body are just as radical. Most of these changes take place during the ages of 12-14. This age level has been given the title of Junior High by both the sacred and secular educators. Educators in the secular field have separated the younger adolescent from the older adolescent. The Junior High school is of rather recent vintage and covers grades seven, eight, and nine. The graded Sunday school assigns the same grade levels to the 12-14 year old student. Here, he is sometimes called an Intermediate.

Every child has an inner time clock that governs the developmental process. The endocrine glands are responsible for the transformations within the child's body. There is sufficient evidence from experiments that have been conducted to prove that the function of the endocrine glands is influenced by both heredity and environment.

In this book we can only deal with the generalities or the norms. It has been stated repeatedly that there are exceptions to every normal pattern. This is especially true in establishing growth norms. There will always be variances. It takes boys longer to attain their mature height than it does girls. The average American woman of today is 65 to 66 inches tall. She usually reaches this height at 14 years of age. From then until 18 years of age the gain in height is at a very slow pace. After 18 years of age there is seldom any gain. The average American boy measures 69.5 inches at 18 years. Boys continue to grow until they are 21 or 22.[2]

The Junior High student will naturally gain weight during this growth spurt. The additonal weight will come from the bones growing larger as well as heavier. A pronounced increase in muscle tissue will also account for weight increase. All of the vital organs of the body (these also have a high muscle content) are also increasing in size as the body changes inwardly and as it changes outwardly.

In both sexes, the arms, legs, and neck grow faster than the head and trunk during early adolescence. This gives these young people their long-legged, gawky look. Facial hair and chest hair appear on boys and are considered a mark of manhood. Girls may develop a slight mustache and a sprinkling of facial hair.

In boys and girls alike, the skin becomes coarser, with larger pores. The sebaceous glands become more active and produce an oily secretion. These factors contribute to the problems of acne and blackheads that plague so many young people. The sweat glands also become more active. Adolescents are self-conscious about these matters. They have become special targets of advertising for deodorants and skin ointments.

An Explanation. Adolescence is also the period of development to sexual maturity. When puberty is completed the young adolescent will be physically capable of reproduction. Every Sunday school teacher needs to know and understand the process of sexual maturation. The sexual development of the adolescent will not be discussed in this book. This book is designed to be taught as a study course before mixed groups of varying ages. If the subject of sexual maturation were discussed in some of the following paragraphs some would say that this book is too frank. Failure to discuss the subject will bring the accusation of being prudish. The latter course has been decided upon so the latter accusation is correct. Every teacher of Junior High and Senior High pupils ought to be as widely read on this subject as possible. They will come to understand their pupils more fully by doing so.

The Junior High youth will not have the excessive energy he possessed as a Junior. He will tire more easily and may be more susceptible to disease, especially the common cold. He may experience pains in various parts of the body. These have been accurately called "growing pains." Some of these pains are associated with puberty while others may be associated with the stretching of the muscles and the growth of the bones.

The Junior child doesn't care too much about bathing. Now that he is an adolescent the idea may occur to him that he needs a bath and bathing will become more frequent. The adolescent has become aware of his appearance. Hours may be spent before the mirror in primping. Clothes are now of concern, especially in wearing whatever is in vogue.

THE CHANGING MENTALITY

Identity. G. Stanley Hall (1844-1924) was the first psychologist to advance a psychology of adolescence. He bridged the past with the present. Hall described adolescence as a period of *Sturm und Drang,* "storm and stress." Hall perceived the emotional life of the adolescent as oscilating between conflicting tendencies.[3]

Hall is revered in psychology circles because he was the man who earned America's first Ph.D. in psychology and was the founder of the child study movement in the United States. To better understand Hall's viewpoint, the following section is quoted from an article by Albert Bundura that appeared in the book, *Studies in Adolescence,*

> The adolescent presumably is engaged in a struggle to emancipate himself from his parents. He, therefore, resists any dependence upon them for their guidance, approval or company, and rebels against any restrictions and controls that they impose upon his behavior. To facilitate the process of emancipation, he transfers his dependency to the peer group whose values are typically in conflict with those of his parents.[4]

Hall believed that these conflicting values contributed to the inner-stress of the adolescent. Further inner-conflict stemmed from the fact that the adolescent is neither child nor adult and is casting about, trying to find his own identity.

Hall's theories do not totally survive the scrutiny of research. For example it has been found that by the time a child reaches adolescence he has pretty well internalized the parents' values and standards to a large degree. Further studies have revealed that the child has emancipated himself from his parents prior to adolescence rather than during this period. In the previous chapter we discovered that the Junior child rejected adult leadership in favor of his peer group. Most adolescents choose friends who share similar value systems and behavioral norms. The peer group helps to reinforce these values and standards. The Biblical statement of Proverbs 22:6 is correct, "Train up a child in the way he should go: and when he is old, he will not depart from it."

Hall was correct in the aspect that the adolescent has difficulty in trying to find his own identity. As has been pointed out, the adolescent is physically mature but mentally immature. Adolescence in our present society has lengthened out. This has not always been so. Shakespeare's Juliet was only fourteen. In colonial times, marriages often took place in the early teens. There seems to be little doubt that today's teen-ager is totally unprepared for marriage. This lack of preparation is more the result of our present culture than heredity.

The adolescent is age conscious. Most twelve-year-olds are quite anxious to reach thirteen. They would rather be identified as almost thirteen than as twelve. Adolescents want to wear clothes that make them look older. They have learned from childhood play that "dressing up" does make one look older than anything else one can do. Snow caps and mittens are replaced by hats, scarves, and gloves. Bobby socks are replaced by nylons. We can now understand Dr. Rolf's definition of adolescence for he told us "adolescence is a period in which new adjustments have to be made, namely those that distinguish child behavior from adult behavior in a given society." It is as though the adolescent is holding hands with himself as a Junior on one side and as a young adult on the other side.

Dr. Clarence H. Benson divided the adolescent years into two groups, early adolescence, embracing the years from thirteen to sixteen and later adolescence, embracing the years from seventeen to twenty. Dr. Benson states that the early adolescent is neither child nor man and thus is a complex of contradictions.[5]

Mentally and Emotionally. The Junior High student will not lose his excellent memory he possessed as a Junior. He may consider Bible memory work to be childish. He must have a purpose now for memorizing Scripture and there is no better motivation than that of witnessing. He is now capable of thinking more deeply than ever before. He is reasonable, but must have a reason for accepting the truths that are taught him. He is now ready to move from the concrete to the abstract.

The early adolescent will make snap judgments. He may be fickle in his likes and dislikes. He may judge someone as not being his "type" one week and become a bosom buddy of that individual the following week. He is quick to judge another by his own standards and has very little sympathy for anyone who makes a mistake. He will judge an entire group of people by the actions of one person in the group. The young adolescent is a thinker but his thinking is often immature.

The young adolescent is a daydreamer. His increased mentality makes daydreaming a more pleasurable experience than it was in childhood. His imagination does not carry him to fairyland as it did as a child. His imagination as an adolescent involves reality. In his daydream he becomes the star of the football team. He is the quarterback and is racing down the field to score the touchdown while the crowd cheers wildly. He may dream of himself as being the most popular boy in school. All of the girls are attracted to him and he is elected the president of the student body. Daydreaming can be a pleasant form of recreation. It can become dangerous when it becomes a continuous escape from reality and if the daydreamer receives a distorted concept of himself and his abilities.

The young adolescent may face some problems with his self-confidence. He may try to cover up a lack of self-confidence by a braggadocious or boisterous attitude. The adolescent who can accept himself will have confidence to carry out successfully what he undertakes and to get along well with those of the same age. When his peers realize that he has confidence in himself, they will have greater confidence in and respect for him. It is important then that the Sunday school teacher contribute in every way possible to the building of a favorable self-concept.

THE CHANGING SOCIALITY

Hurlock states that socialization "is the process of learning to conform to group standards, mores, and customs. It is the ability to behave in accordance with social expectations." Socialization is a cultural process. The process is quite different in the different societies of the world. One only needs to compare the societies of the Apache, the Arab, and the American to discover the marked differences in socialization. Our concern is with the socialization of the American adolescent and we will find descriptive patterns that help us arrive at conclusions about this socialization.

The Adolescent's Parents. The adolescent may not be the chief cause for his period of life being described as one of stress and storm. Much of the stress and storm may come from the fact that parents do not understand the transition that is taking place in their child. Thus the adolescent is sometimes correct in his charge, "No one understands me." Further confict may stem from the wrong kind of power structure in the home.

There are three types of power structures in the home. When the mother has the final say in family matters and on child-rearing policies then the family is said to be a matriarchy. When the father is dominant in these roles then the family is said to be a patriarchal family. In an equalitarian family, parents are seen as sharing the power throughout.[6]

Research has revealed that dominance on the part of either mother or father in child-rearing relations is strongly associated with parental rejection. The highest efforts in adolescent achievement are scored by those teen-agers who come from equalitarian family structures.

Little has been said about the home in any previous chapters of this broad treatment of growth and development. The home is still the basic unit of society. When the home becomes decadent then society becomes decadent. The discussion in the previous paragraphs reveals that child-rearing requires a team-effort on the part of both parents. The day-by-day rearing of the children rests mainly on the mother's shoulders, but both the mother and father must be together in their philosophy of child-rearing. This is a complex problem, but it is not a problem that cannot be resolved by good Christian parents.

Parental-adolescent conflict can stem from problems in the home, especially when there is constant bickering in the home. Conflict can also arise when parents fail to accept the adolescent for what he is. Some parents do not want their children to become adults and thus they do all they can to retard maturation. Other parents want their children to become adults as soon as they reach puberty. The result of either of these positions can be conflict. The adolescent is not a freak. He is going through the normal changes that every human being passes through. Wise parents will be patient and understanding with their adolescents. They will understand that their son or daughter is casting about and seeking an identity. They will further understand that they can make a strong contribution in building their child's self-confidence. The Sunday school teacher will find it quite difficult to cope with some of the problems that are created in the home.

The Adolescent's Peers. We have already determined that the adolescent is strongly affected by his culture. The social strata of his parents will greatly influence the socialization of the adolescent. There are degrees of variation in the socialization of adolescents from the lower class, middle class, and upper class societies of our nation. Once more we will only deal with what is considered to be the norms as they cross the invisible barriers of one society level or another. There is the danger of branding the adolescent who does not measure up to the norms as being abnormal. There will always be exceptions to the rule. Norms are arrived at by compiling averages. There are always variances in these averages.

The gangs of childhood gradually disappear during early adolescence. The adolescent becomes more selective in the choice of his friends and tends to have fewer friendships than he had as a child. Hurlock states that adolescents divide their friends into three groupings: their chums, their cliques, and their crowds. Chums or pals are the adolescent's inseparable companions and confidants. They tend to dress alike and spend as much time together as possible. When they cannot be together they will spend as much time together on the telephone as their parents will allow.

A clique is made of individuals who are brought together daily. A clique will usually contain three or more individuals of similar interests. Most cliques of early adolescence only include those of the same sex. In middle adolescence the clique widens to include those of both sexes. Most cliques are formed at school. Some are formed as a result of recreational activities while others are formed at church. An adolescent can easily move about in several cliques. There are numerous advantages and disadvantages that are gained by the adolescent and his participation in the clique.

The crowd is the outer circle of the adolescent's social group. The crowd meets on the basis of activities and these activities are usually carried out away from home. Generally, the crowd has a meeting place that is called "the hangout." It may be a drugstore, an ice cream shop, or a street corner. The crowd meets to participate in social activities, to talk, and to eat. The crowd may participate in skating, bowling, watching athletic contests or other activities that meet their mutual interest. The topics of their conversation will vary from intimate personal matters to rather broad political or social problems. A crowd meeting is never complete without eating. The crowd will want to eat whatever appeals to them rather than what is good for them. There are advantages and disadvantages to be gained from socialization with the crowd.[7]

Conformity appears to be the standard pattern for all adolescents, especially early adolescents. The opinions of those who are one's own age now become extremely important. In order to conform to the group the adolescent will often accept opinions that he disagrees with or disapproves of. Conformity especially appears in the manner of dress and fads. Adolescents will dress alike, talk alike, and act alike. In his search for role identity the adolescent derives a sense of security from conformity to the role played by his peers. The individual will only accept innovations when they fit the framework of teen culture. Adolescents fail to realize that much of their culture in this modern world originates in the fertile brain of adults. Adults have learned that there is a tremendous financial market among teen-agers. Every town or city has its radio station that beams its message to teen-agers. Magazines and newspapers are geared toward the teen-age market.

The Adolescent's Puppy Love. At the time that World War One ended, the median age for beginning to date was 16 years. Today, it is 14 years, although some boys and girls have their first dates earlier than 14. Some parents thrust their children or adolescents toward early dating as they want their youngsters to be socially acceptable to the opposite sex. Most adolescents reserve regular dating for the years beyond Junior High but many of them have experienced several cases of "puppy love" by that time. In most situations puppy love surfaces in unusual ways of showing interest in each other. It takes the form of wisecracking, teasing, and even rough-housing. Intimacies such as hand holding and kissing are usually reserved for daydreaming.

Adolescents live in a present-day society that encourages early dating but discourages early marriages. Early dating should be discouraged in favor of group activities. Serious courtships should be reserved for the years of later adolescence.

The Adolescent's Problems. Today's adolescent faces unique problems. He wants to be accepted by his peers but this drive for acceptance can lead to trouble and the adolescent could become a juvenile delinquent.

The term—juvenile delinquent—is difficult to define. In America the range of juvenile delinquency varies from state to state. It may range from serious crimes such as murder, burglary, or robbery to such trivial acts as playing ball in the street, building a tree house in a public park, or obstructing traffic on a sidewalk.

Juvenile courts have been established in every state

to cope with juvenile problems. These courts generally deal with the adolescent who has not achieved his eighteenth birthday. When the adolescent passes his eighteenth birthday, his unlawful act is passed on to the adult courts. Most juvenile courts are more lenient than their adult counterparts.

Each year more than 700,000 boys and girls appear before juvenile courts for nontraffic offenses. It is estimated that approximately one in every nine youths will be referred to the juvenile court before his eighteenth birthday. In addition, many minor offenders are handled directly by the police and never appear before the courts. Most of the offenders are boys. For every one girl brought to the attention of the juvenile courts, there are four or five boys.

Most juvenile offenders do not become adult criminals. If they did, each state would have to increase the size of its penal institutions. It has been proven that the confirmed delinquent becomes a confirmed criminal. The Sunday school and the church *must* fulfill their responsibility in reaching the hard-core delinquent as well as the first offender.

Drug addiction or usage has become a problem for today's adolescent. In 1958, 12 percent of the drug cases known to the Federal Bureau of Narcotics were under age 21. The current problem of drug addition claims the attention of the President of the nation as well as the parents of every teen-ager. The percentage of adolescent drug users increases each year. Many of the juvenile court problems today are drug related. Every Sunday school worker should join in an active campaign against drug usage. Every Intermediate Sunday school teacher should be well acquainted with the problems of drug use and abuse. The younger adolescent should be made aware of the evils of drug experimentation and usage.[8]

THE CHANGING SPIRITUALITY

Many publishing houses do not sell the volume of literature for Intermediates that they do for Juniors. The explanation is that adolescents begin to drift in their search for identity. Many churches allow them to gravitate away from the church with very little effort to retain them. Much competition is offered for the attention of the adolescent and the church must not withdraw from that competition. Some churches mistakenly try to enter into this competition by offering the same attractions as their competitors. Adolescents do not expect nor respect this approach. The discussion that follows will help us to better understand adolescents and their changing spirituality.

The Adolescent's Faith. It is a common opinion that today's adolescents are "going to the dogs." The rise in juvenile delinquency would seem to indicate this. However, in a nationwide poll of high school students, it was found that there is very little agnosticism and almost no atheism. A survey conducted by H. H. Remmers and D. H. Radler has revealed the following general characteristics about the adolescent's religious life:

The typical American teenager today retains a favorable attitude toward the church, attends services about once a week and says prayers once or twice a day.

His religious beliefs usually agree with those of his parents.

He thinks of God as an omnipotent and omniscient bodiless spirit who exists everywhere.

He feels that his prayers are sometimes answered.

He believes in the hereafter and expects his place there to be determined by his conduct here on earth.

He believes that God guided or inspired the writing of the Bible.[9]

It is evident that the adolescent has advanced in his understanding from the concrete to the abstract. He is now capable of real thinking about Deity and will welcome the challenge to do so. Even though he is now capable of understanding theology he is not interested in it. He is more concerned about practical Christianity that will help him in his daily life. Many adolescents now show a keener interest in the worship hour than they do the Sunday school hour. This is especially true if the Sunday school hour is dull and meaningless. Before this chapter is concluded some discussion will be presented as to how to make the Sunday school hour more meaningful for the Intermediate.

The Adolescent's Doubts. Doubting may begin in childhood but it normally reaches its peak in adolescence. The sources of doubt may be multiple. The fact that the adolescent is encouraged to think independently can result in doubt. He may find conflict in what he has been taught in Sunday school with what he is being taught in Junior High. The adolescent may encounter friends with different religious beliefs and he will begin to wonder which beliefs are correct. This will especially be true if his own religion places certain taboos on certain forms of behavior that are permitted in other religions.

Insincerity in the lives of adults can be another source of doubt for the adolescent. Adolescents are casting about for an ideal and they are quick to spot a phony. They are given to snap-judgment which is sometimes erroneous, but too often their judgment is correct.

The Adolescent Drop-Out. Studies of church and Sunday school attendance have shown that there is a gradual decrease in attendance as the adolescent years progress. This fact may seem to contradict the statement that very few adolescents are agnostic or atheistic.

The statement is reconciled though when one discovers that while adolescents maintain an active faith in God at the same time they lose interest in church attendance. The older adolescent does not believe that church attendance is necessary to help him lead a good life. More will be said about this matter in the next chapter.

THE JUNIOR HIGH YOUTH IN RETROSPECT

The onset of adolescence brings with it the start of maturation. Begun at puberty, adolescence covers almost all, if not all, of the teen years. The body of the adolescent is changing rapidly on the inside as well as on the outside. Adolescence has been called the "age of storm and stress" by some psychologists. Admittedly the adolescent is casting about as he seeks his identity, but a child who has proper guidance through adolescence will become a well-rounded adult. The Sunday school teacher can act as a guide along this path.

THE INTERMEDIATE TEACHER

There will be the temptation for some teachers to turn through the pages of this book and find the chapter that relates to their interest in teaching. This is much like the person who reads the last chapter of a mystery story first. Each of these chapters is a building block erected upon the foundation of the introduction. One will be a better informed teacher if he reads the whole book. Something said to one level of teaching can well be adapted and applied to another level. Various aspects of teacher training are woven throughout this book; another important aspect follows.

AN INTRODUCTION TO
METHODS OF TEACHING

The dictionary defines a method as "a way of doing anything; especially a regular, orderly, definite procedure or way of teaching." Every Sunday school teacher uses some method in teaching. The tragedy lies in the fact that many Sunday school teachers consistently use the same method of teaching Sunday after Sunday, year after year.

One of the problems that many teachers have failed to realize is that they have not taught until the pupil has learned. Some teachers believe that teaching is funneling words into their listeners' ears. The problem with this theory is that the receiver may not be tuned in though the station continues to broadcast.

The Sunday school teacher is teaching for a purpose. First, he must recognize and accept his responsibility to lead each pupil to trust in Christ and accept Him as personal Saviour. Secondly, the teacher is to present the eternal purpose of God. The more abundant Christian life is the theme of the Christian teacher. Thirdly, the Sunday school teacher is to direct and guide each pupil to fulfill God's will in his life. God has a plan for every Christian. His Word gives directions for knowing His will. The teacher instructs his pupils in the realities of Christian growth.

Once the teacher has realized some aims and objectives for his teaching he has won half the battle, but only half the battle. The wise teacher will then seek for a variety of methods in teaching in order to achieve his aims and objectives. How many different methods are there? They are innumerable. A good Sunday school teacher will be in constant search for some new method in which to present his lesson material. A sanctified imagination will be creative in producing new ideas and methods.

The Choice of a Method. The teacher does not want to get bogged down with a decision as to which method of teaching to use. There are certain guidelines that might be used in deciding upon a particular method. One of these is the goals to be achieved. Of course we have already determined what these goals are. We are striving to bring about change. We want to bring about changes in knowing. The ultimate goal is for each pupil to come to know the Lord Jesus Christ as his own personal Saviour. We want to bring about changes in feeling. The pupil is brought into the concept of the eternal purpose of God. We want to bring about changes in doing. This is the crux of all Sunday school teaching. We are striving to change each pupil's life into one patterned after that of Christ. With a knowledge of these goals in mind we can more properly select the correct method for lesson presentation.

Here are other factors that will help determine the type of method you may choose:

1. The size of the group to be taught. The small group is preferred because it is easier to create an atmosphere of interaction between the teacher and the pupils. When the class is large, the best methods to be used are those that require one-way communication, or where the audience is divided into smaller groups before or after some more general presentation of information.

2. The size of the room in which your class meets. Churches should keep methodology in mind when they design and build their educational units. Ideally these should be informal rooms with adaptable equipment such as movable seating. Projection equipment as well as chalkboards will be needed to be used as a part of, if not all of, some methods to be used.

3. The time that is available. Generally speaking, more time is required when the group members are involved in two-way communication.

4. The resources that are available. Resources may include educational aids such as audio-visual materials, a large variety of printed materials, and various resource persons.

5. The proximity of other groups. The noise factor as well as the sight factor may affect other groups and hence limit your methods of teaching.

6. The age of the class members. As age increases, the rate of mobility declines. Some methods are used with children while others are more adaptable to adults.

7. The climate of your class. You will need to consider the cultural, ethnic, educational, psychological, sociological and spiritual climate of your class. It is therefore important for the teacher to know his students.

8. The teacher himself. The ability of the teacher will help determine the methods used although the teacher should be willing to venture forth into new methods. If a new way of teaching is well planned and well executed, its use will be rewarding to you and the members of your class. If you do not succeed

the first time—try again![10]

Thus far we have explored the factors that will help us decide upon a method to use. In the next chapter we will examine a partial list of some methods that can be used effectively.

CONCLUSION

The Junior High teacher has a most difficult task. He must help shape a life while it is still pliable. If he fails more than a life may be lost—a soul may be lost forever. A well-trained Junior High teacher will win his unsaved class members to Christ and help guide them into Christian maturity.

CHAPTER SIX

FOOTNOTES

[1] Rolf E. Muuss, *Theories of Adolescence* (New York, 1968), p. 4.

[2] Elizabeth B. Hurlock, *Adolescent Development* (New York, 1967), p. 42.

[3] Muuss, pp. 34-35.

[4] Robert E. Grinder, ed., *Studies in Adolescence* (Toronto, 1969), p. 17.

[5] Clarence H. Benson, *An Introduction to Child Study* (Chicago, 1942), p. 173.

[6] Grinder, p. 110.

[7] Hurlock, p. 123.

[8] Ruth Shonle Cavon, *Juvenile Delinquency, Development-Treatment-Control* (Philadelphia, 1969), pp. 8-9.

[9] Hurlock, p. 392.

[10] Martha M. Leypoldt, *40 Ways To Teach in Groups* (Valley Forge, 1967), pp. 25-36.

CHAPTER SIX

QUESTIONS FOR REVIEW

1. List the ages of the Junior High student as well as the corresponding grades for the graded Sunday school.

2. When does adolescence begin? What time period does it normally cover?

3. Explain the "storm and stress" opinion of some psychologists.

4. What is a good motivator that might prod the adolescent on to memorize Bible passages?

5. What unit of society is basic and contributes to the rise or fall of society?

6. Hurlock lists three groupings for the adolescent's friends. Define each.

7. What blanket term is given to describe criminal activities of adolescents?

8. Do statistics agree with the statement that "all teen-agers are going to the dogs"? Explain your answer.

9. List the triune purpose of the Sunday school teacher.

10. List the factors one must consider in selecting a method of teaching.

CHAPTER SEVEN

THE SENIOR HIGH YOUTH

This chapter continues our survey begun in the previous chapter for the Senior High level—ages 15-17—continues the progressive development of the adolescent. The Senior High pupil has already developed physically and will develop further emotionally and mentally during these years of his life. Like the Junior High pupil the Senior High pupil has the same title in both the sacred and secular fields of education. The graded Sunday school assigns the same grade levels as the Senior High school—grades ten, eleven, and twelve.

Many educators and psychologists separate adolescence into three periods. The Junior High youth is called an early adolescent, the Senior High youth is called a middle adolescent, and the young adult is the later adolescent. The Young Adult will be discussed in the next chapter.

Some early psychologists argue that an unstable psychological environment during adolescence brings about instability in an individual. Kurt Lewin, who was a pupil of the Gestalt school at the University of Berlin, held that "behavior is a function of the person and his environment." His formula reads $B=f(PE)$.[1]

It is true that one's environment will greatly affect an adolescent but so will his environment during the other periods of maturity. It must be remembered that by the time one progresses to adulthood his life has been molded by a variety of experiences throughout childhood and adolescence. A traumatic experience in any one period may have lasting effects throughout one's life. By the time one reaches middle adolescence his life patterns are pretty well determined.

FURTHER PHYSICAL DEVELOPMENT

A Slower Pace. The growth rate will generally slow down during middle adolescence. The physical awkwardness of the previous period begins to disappear. In early adolescence the girls have a tendency to grow faster than boys. Most girls reach their adult height by the time they reach sixteen. Boys will continue to "push up" until they are twenty-one. Their growth rate will usually be much slower now than it was during early adolescence.

The adolescent's body is extremely important to him. The body is the capsule in which the soul is temporarily enclosed. We are more concerned with the soul but we must not overlook the importance of the body. Doors do open more easily to attractive young people. Beautiful girls have greater opportunities to become cheerleaders or occupy other roles of leadership in school. Strong, athletic boys are more readily received at school. They become the heroes of younger and older of his peers and adult leaders.

There are definite social hazards in one being too

beautiful or too handsome. When success comes too easily to the adolescent he may expect success to come as easily in the long haul of life.

A Sound Body. Adolescents need good physical fitness programs. The body that tired easily during early adolescence will now burst forth with energy. The desire for food will wane some. The need of proper sleep is just as great during middle adolescence as early adolescence. Most upper teens usually believe they can get by with less sleep than before but this opinion is untrue. A loss of sleep can be a hindrance to study. Many Senior High pupils yawn and nap through the Sunday school hour because of loss of sleep the previous night.

In our discussion we are still following the scriptural account of the development of the Lord Jesus. Remember it was said of Jesus that He "increased in wisdom and stature, and in favour with God and man." One must grow spiritually! One must grow physically at the same time. The young person who takes care of his body and recognizes it as the temple of the Holy Spirit will have little difficulty in growing in the Spirit and in favor with God.

The average American girl is 5 feet 5 inches tall. The female ideal is that she is petite with small hands and feet, a slender body, and a non-athletic appearance. The average American male is 5 feet 10 inches tall. The ideal for him is that he is strong, broad-shouldered, and well developed in muscle. Some young people go to great lengths to achieve these ideals. Girls will diet and refrain from exercise. Boys will lift weights and perform other strenuous exercises. Some adolescents are caused a great deal of anguish because they do not measure up to the ideals of their sex. Boys become concerned if they are short and lacking in strength. Sometimes they overcompensate for their size by developing an authoritarian personality. Girls become concerned if they are overweight. Sometimes they overcompensate by developing a prowess in various types of athletics that are usually dominated by the male. A dissatisfaction with their bodies can cause damaging psychological effects.

Some adolescents have physical defects. The defect may be minor such as a broken front tooth, a small scar on the face, or bad eye sight corrected by thick lensed glasses. The defect may be major and resultant from birth or an accident. Such defects add to the difficulty of adjustment during adolescence. Obesity may be a problem. Someone has said, "It is bad enough to be fat and forty, but to be fat and fourteen is still harder to bear." Contrary to the popular opinion, fat boys and girls are not always happy boys and girls. Overt action may not truthfully reflect covert attitudes.

A Good Appearance. The middle adolescent will be all the more concerned about his appearance. His interest in the opposite sex now goes beyond daydreaming and dating will begin. The necessary steps will be taken that makes one more attractive to the opposite sex. He will be more concerned about his appearance in the eyes of his peers than he will in the eyes of his parents. There may be strong disagreement between parents and their adolescents as to what constitutes neat appearance.

FURTHER MENTAL DEVELOPMENT

The Time Factor. An important factor in adolescent development is the enlargement and conceptualization of the time perspective. The young child lives mainly in the present; the past and the future include only a few days or weeks and have little effect on his behavior. During the adolescent period the time concept develops so that the past becomes significant to the adolescent. The future also becomes more meaningful. The adolescent begins to plan his life and set his goals. He has to make choices in his training and prepare for a vocation. These decisions especially arise during middle adolescence.[2]

The Knowledge Factor. William Willkens discusses educational development in modern times in his book titled, *The Youth Years*. He states:

> Modern young people live in a world of education that would have overpowered youth of an earlier period if they had been suddenly thrust into it. For example, ninth

graders are studying levels of biology covered only in college classes a few years ago, and groups of high school seniors study courses that are clearly classed as college-level. In these days young people are discovering worlds of knowledge almost too fantastic to comprehend.[3]

Have you tried to help your children with their homework recently? Parents who are college graduates are finding the homework of their offspring difficult to comprehend. The new math has confused many mothers and fathers. Language is learned in a laboratory with the use of tape recorders and other devices. Teaching machines, which give each student the opportunity to proceed at his own speed, are used. Team teaching allows experts in their field to present classroom material.

Most young people today have the advantage of a high school education. Enrollment in colleges has more than doubled in the last decade. The following table provides an interesting comparison of present high school youth and their forefathers.

Year	All Schools	Public Schools	Non-Public School Totals	Percent of 14-17 Age-group
1889-90	359,949	202,963	94,931	6.7
1919-20	2,500,176	2,200,389	213.920	32.3
1929-30	4,804,255	4,399,422	341,158	51.4
1939-40	7,123,009	6,635,337	487,672	73.3
1949-50	6,453,009	5,757,810	695,199	76.8
1959-60	9,599,810	8,531,454	1,068,356	86.1
1963-64	12,600,000	11,200,000	1,400,000	93.5

Table 1. U.S. School Enrollment in Grades 9-12, 1889-90 to 1963-64[4]

In light of the above information is it any wonder that the high school youth becomes bored with Sunday school when the same methods are practiced that were used back in the days of his grandparents? We do not need to change the subject matter—the Bible—but we do need to incorporate some new methods and new approaches in teaching the Bible.

The Nature-Nurture Factor. For years psychologists have argued concerning the more important contributor to one's I.Q.—heredity or environment. Research has proven both factors to be important. There is no doubt that heredity is important in determining intellectual development. Longitudinal studies suggest that environment may make the difference between I.Q. averages as low as 80 or 85 to as high as 115. There is no spurt in intellectual growth during adolescence. As has been pointed out conceptual growth does take place and is fully developed by the end of adolescence.[5]

The Bible I.Q. of many Senior High youth is extremely low. Many fail simple Bible tests given to them. Does this mean that those who attend Sunday school and church are of a lower mentality? Of course not. It may well be that the high school youth has progressed through the various levels of Sunday school without being taught. Teaching is more than telling. The teacher has not taught until the pupil has learned. Teaching is compared to brick-laying. One course is laid upon the other. Each course rests upon the foundation. No brick mason starts in the middle and works down or up. Many well-trained and concerned Senior High teachers find it difficult to "lay their course" because some predecessor did not lay his course properly. In some instances no foundation was laid. The Sunday school needs more than one well-trained teacher; it needs a well-trained staff.

FURTHER SOCIAL DEVELOPMENT

In the previous chapter we observed that the adolescent divides his friends into three groupings, his chums, his clique, and his crowd. In middle adolescence the clique is widened to include both sexes. In middle adolescence boys tend to have a wider circle of friends while girls have fewer and deeper friendships. Many of the friendships of this period become lifelong relationships.

The Dating Age. There is a strong emphasis on dating during middle adolescence. "Going steady" becomes a regular pattern although partners are changed frequently. Dating is made easier by access to an automobile. Most young people participate in driver's training during their Senior High years. If they bypass this means then they are taught to drive by some member of the family or some friend. Many Senior High boys own their own automobile. The automobile has become a status symbol among teen-agers. It remains a status symbol for adults.

The Mating Age. After a few dates a boy and girl may decide to "go steady." The girl accepts the boy's high school ring. By means of a piece of wax or string the ring-size is adjusted to fit the girl. Most young people experience a number of steadies before they finally select their lifemate.

The Sunday school classroom provides a good arena for discussion about dating. Since most boys and girls are interested in dating why not discuss such topics as, "Should Christians date non-Christians?" "Where can Christian teens go on dates?" and "What about hand-holding and kissing?" Some Senior High teachers believe that such discussions are out of place in Sunday school. However, with proper guidance and prudence such topics as those listed above can be highly beneficial.

The Sunday school class can become a means of social activity for the Senior High pupil. The teacher who is willing to go the second mile in planning good wholesome social activities for his class will be well rewarded.

The Independent Age. The middle adolescent will spend less time at home. He will spend more time with his peers or his date. As stated above the automobile or motor "bike" provides him with mobility. He may spend his time "just riding around" with friends. The automobile will allow him to travel greater distances to sports events. He may even go to a friend's house to do his homework.

Dr. Clarence Benson states that "parents must recognize the growing spirit of independence which is as natural to this stage as dependence is to the child."[6] The rule by authority must give way to the rule by reason. Some parents err in attempting to keep their adolescents dependent. If they are ever to leave the nest and make a home of their own then adolescents must be allowed degrees of independence. The degrees of independence will be determined by each individual adolescent rather than by some sliding scale that permits degrees of independence because one has reached a certain age.

The School Age. The school one attends will provide opportunities for socialization. The school becomes a source of friends and shared activities—athletic contests, plays, and special-interest clubs. The adolescent will select his chums, cliques, and crowds from school. Some high schools have introduced sororities and fraternities to facilitate socialization. Some group activities are excellent in that they keep young people out of mischief. Some group activities only serve to promote mischief.

The school has a distinct advantage over the church. Schooling will occupy most of the time of an adolescent. He spends an average of thirty hours per week in the classroom. He spends a portion of his time doing his homework. The church only has the adolescent for a few hours each week. The responsible persons *must* make these hours count as much as possible.

The Christian School. Private schools are flourishing today. Some churches have had parochial schools for years but in the last few years many fundamental churches have begun their own program for education. In these schools secular education is blended with sacred. The Bible is taught as a portion of the curriculum. Students have the advantage of being taught by teachers who are Christians. Most of their peers are Christians. These schools provide a wholesome program of socialization for the adolescent.

FURTHER SPIRITUAL DEVELOPMENT

A survey conducted among Senior High school youth of one particular denomination revealed that about two-thirds of the young people were bothered by religious doubt and uncertainty. Another two-thirds were bothered about an uncertainty in their relationship to God. About forty-three percent craved a deeper faith in God.[7]

In 1968 Dr. Roy Zuck and Dr. Gene Getz

completed a youth study for the National Sunday School Association. Questionnaires were sent out to some 3,000 teen-agers of evangelical churches. The statistics compiled from this survey are perhaps the most thorough available today. They can be found in a book entitled, *Christian Youth, An In-Depth Study.* A copy of this book should be in your church library. In the paragraphs that follow we shall glean some facts from this book about the Senior High youth's spiritual development.

Church Attendance. Studies of church and Sunday school attendance have shown that there is a gradual decrease in attendance as the adolescent years progress. Hurlock lists some of the reasons given by adolescents for not attending church. They are:

1. Failure of parents to attend.
2. Lack of interesting services.
3. Being forced to attend when they were younger.
4. The attitude of the church toward different forms of recreation.
5. The church does little to make membership meaningful to young people.
6. Too much emphasis on doctrinal and denominational differences.
7. Formalism and meaningless traditionalism that clutter up the services.[8]

It would be well if each Senior High school teacher

would check this list of gripes and see what contribution they might make to improve the situation.

Prayer. In the Christian youth survey that was conducted among evangelical youth it was learned that only 15.5 percent of these young people were satisfied with their prayer life. Some 43.7 percent were dissatisfied while some 40.6 percent reported that they had no strong feeling either way. Most of those who were questioned indicated that they prayed daily.[9]

Bible Reading. While a good percentage of young people pray every day, the highest percentage of them do not read their Bibles daily. Approximately one-fourth of those who were surveyed read their Bibles daily while some 10 to 15 percent admitted to never reading their Bibles. It is interesting to observe that the older adolescent read his Bible more than the younger adolescent. This would conflict with the opinion of some that the adolescent is on a slide downward. Of course it must be remembered that the youth survey was conducted among teen-agers who go to church. Surveys among drop-outs would reveal different statistics.

Giving. The youth survey discovered that many young people of high school age are working part-time. About one-third of those surveyed who have an income from part-time work or an allowance are giving 10 percent or more of their income to the Lord's work. Good stewardship practices should have been established in earlier years. It is not too late to encourage good stewardship during adolescence.

Church Vocations. Many Senior High youth discover and determine the Lord's will for their lives during these years of middle adolescence. Some young people are misled into the belief that the only way they can serve the Lord is to be a missionary or pastor. Church related vocations are broad and widening every year. The discussion in this area will be enlarged in the next chapter.

THE SENIOR HIGH YOUTH IN RETROSPECT

The Senior High youth is beginning to find himself. For the past few years he has been seeking for his identity. He is now beginning to mature. He is healthy and has a keen mind. He is now more interested in the opposite sex than he has ever been before. He can now develop into a mature Christian and may show signs of leadership ability. This ability should be cultivated to the utmost.

THE SENIOR HIGH TEACHER

This well-trained teacher will have a blessed ministry. Most of his pupils will be Christians. He will have the opportunity to guide his pupils toward Christian maturity. He can assist in unfolding the Lord's will for every class member. It is blessed to win a soul to Christ; it is also blessed to help someone grow in the grace and knowledge of the Lord Jesus Christ. This can be done by making the Sunday school hour lively and vital. A variety of methods will help you accomplish your goals. We shall now continue our study of methods that was introduced in the last chapter. This study will be completed in the next and final chapter.

A VARIETY OF METHODS

Space will not permit an investigation into all of the methods that have been catalogued. With the passing of time new methods are discovered as some are tied in with scientific discovery. A prime example of this is the tape cassette. In the very near future you will be able to view the speaker as well as hear him on cassette and a whole avenue of new methods will be opened.

The Lecture Method. Since the most popular method used today is the lecture method we shall explore it first. This method of teaching is erroneously looked upon as the easiest of all the methods and therefore is more widely used than any other one method. In reality this method is very demanding on the teacher as well as the pupil.

The lecturer should be the master of his subject. To become this he must read widely on the subject to be presented. This means that he will read beyond the teacher's quarterly. That teacher who limits his study exclusively to the teacher's quarterly will find himself totally unprepared to lecture. Some confuse this method with the idea of reading a verse of Scripture and then making a few comments before going on to the next verse. This is really Bible exposition and requires many hours of preparation before it can be mastered. Only the thoroughly schooled should attempt Bible exposition lest they become guilty of misrepresenting the Scriptures.

Once the lecturer has read wisely on the subject to be presented he then selects relevent information. He organizes his material into a meaningful outline. He presents the lesson material in a conversational manner. (He is not to preach. Preaching is to be reserved for the preaching hour. To avoid preaching it would be best if the lecturer were seated before his class. He may arise occasionally to refer to some visual but will return to his chair when finished.) The lecturer summarizes the main points of the presentation as he concludes the lesson. He suggests how this information can be used.

In the lecture method the class members are not expected to be completely passive relative to the lesson to be covered. It is true that they are involved in a learning situation that calls for one-way communication but there are still some requirements expected of the class members. The class members are asked to read the material in their pupil's quarterly as well as other required reading materials. The class member listens actively to what the speaker is saying. He may wish to take appropriate notes on the material presented. He will want to associate meanings with previous learning experiences.

The lecture method when properly used can be very effective. The teacher should not overwork this method. Variety should be given to our teaching by using other methods as well. The lecture method should not be used in the children's classes and only sparingly with Intermediates.

The Discussion Method. One of the most ideal methods of teaching is the discussion method. It is recommended for use with the Senior High through Adult groups. In using this technique the teacher assumes the role of a guide in the discussion and hence does not carry on a one-way communication. The discussion method produces pupil reaction by requiring interpretation of the lesson. This prevents the pupil from merely acquiring knowledge without appropriating it. It aids in a continuous development and gradual construction of the lesson and stimulates the spirit of inquiry and personal interest.

The teacher's responsibility is not lessened with the discussion method. The teacher will announce this method in advance and encourage the class members to do independent research prior to the meeting. (This will be done with the pupil's quarterly as well as other resources.) The teacher will want to prepare a series of questions or an outline prior to the meeting to open the discussion. The questions or the outline could be written on the chalkboard as guidelines for the discussion. The teacher will want to arrive early to do this, as well as to prepare the physical setting, with chairs placed around a table so that all class members face one another.

The teacher introduces the problem or lesson to be discussed. He suggests the purpose of the discussion. He presents the outline for the class to follow. The teacher then opens the session for discussion. He will have to guide the class to keep the discussion on track. If a detour is made it should only be done so with the approval of the majority of the class members. The teacher will strive to secure balanced participation from the class members. Over-talkative pupils may want to monopolize the time, not giving opportunity to the retiring person who needs experience in expression. The teacher will want to avoid taking sides and becoming argumentative. He will want to avoid making speeches.

At the conclusion of the lesson the teacher will give a summary and draw the conclusions that have been arrived at through the discussion of the class members. He will suggest avenues of greater study or a course of action.

In spite of the various problems or difficulties that may arise in using this method it is one of the most useful of all teaching methods. It encourages expressional activity and leads pupils to form their own judgments rather than to accept passively or to reject unthinkingly the message of the lesson.

The Circle Response Method. Somewhat similar to the discussion method is the circle response method. In fact there is so much of a similarity that it will only be profitable for us to notice the differences. In this method each of the members of the class is seated in a circle. Each person, in turn, expresses his response to the topic or question to be discussed by the group. No one is allowed to speak a second time until all have a turn. Participants may comment on some other class member's commentary but only when their proper turn in the circle comes.

Buzz Sessions. This method is especially useful with older young people and adults. The class is divided into subgroups of from three to six persons each for a brief period of time, to discuss an assigned topic or to solve a problem. A representative is selected from each subgroup to report its findings to the entire class.

The teacher does not remain passive while the buzz sessions are going on. He gives instructions to each subgroup by defining the task clearly, informing the subgroup members of the time limit to accomplish the task, and suggests that each subgroup select its own leader and recorder. While the subgroups are buzzing the teacher floats from one group to another to determine whether any group needs assistance in performing the task. The teacher gives a two-minute warning signal for subgroups to terminate their task. At the conclusion of the time period allotted he calls the subgroups to reassemble. He then requests a report from each subgroup. Additional comments from any member of the class are welcomed. The teacher then summarizes the findings of the class and lists the conclusions. He suggests additional study or action.

One definite advantage of this method is that it allows opportunity for looking at a number of different facets of the same truth. Another advantage is that it allows for individual participation and contribution which always helps to build interest.[10]

The Panel. Most teachers have become acquainted with the next method by means of television. It is the panel method. In using this method the teacher selects three or four class members prior to the session to serve as a panel, and informs them about the responsibilities they are to assume. The teacher prepares a list of questions he wishes the panel members to consider. He meets with the panel members prior to the meeting to clarify issues and determine the procedure to follow. The class members are encouraged to do independent research prior to the meeting.

The teacher should arrive at Sunday school early enough to set the stage for the panel discussion. A table will be placed in the front of the room with the appropriate number of chairs for the panel members and the teacher. The teacher will introduce the panel members. He will secure participation from all of the panel members and be careful not to inject his own ideas. He may need to clarify some issues. At the close of the session the teacher will summarize the major contributions of the panel members. (He probably should take notes during the session.) He draws conclusions and suggests a course of action or a way to use the information.

There are several ways of varying the panel method. One of these is called the panel forum. This varies from the panel method in that there is free and open discussion among the entire group after the panel has completed their discussion. This will necessitate a briefer discussion period by the panel members in order to give the class members time to discuss the topic or ask questions of the panel members.

Still another method that is akin to the panel method is the symposium. The symposium uses a panel of speakers who are considered to be experts on the subject matter. There are as many panel members as there are aspects of the lesson and each panel member has a certain allotted time in which to speak. He must remain in the framework of his time period or he will infringe on someone else's time. The panel member reads widely on the subject and especially on the aspect of the lesson that has been assigned to him. The teacher's responsibilities remain much the same in the use of this method as those suggested previously for use with the panel.[11]

CONCLUSION

The Senior High teacher is a unique person. He must be genuinely Christian. (Senior Highs can readily spot a phony.) He must be well-trained for the task. (Senior Highs will become bored if he is not.) He must be willing to go the second mile as a teacher. (His rewards will be great if he does.)

The middle adolescent who sits before you today will be a young adult tomorrow. The kind of young adult he will become is partially dependent upon you, the Senior High teacher. This is a great responsibility.

CHAPTER SEVEN

FOOTNOTES

[1] Rolf E. Muuss, *Theories of Adolescence* (New York, 1968), p. 89.

[2] Ibid., p. 103.

[3] William H. R. Willkens, *The Youth Years* (Valley Forge, 1967), pp. 33-34.

[4] Ibid., p. 35.

[5] Boyd R. McCandless, *Adolescents Behavior and Development* (Hinsdale, 1970), p. 257.

[6] Clarence H. Benson, *An Introduction to Child Study* (Chicago, 1945), pp. 182-183.

[7] Willkens, p. 138.

[8] Elizabeth B. Hurlock, *Adolescent Development* (New York, 1967), pp. 409-410.

[9] Roy B. Zuck and Gene Getz, *Christian Youth, An In-Depth Study* (Chicago, 1968), p. 61.

[10] Martha M. Leypoldt, *40 Ways To Teach In Groups* (Valley Forge, 1967), pp. 42-44.

[11] Ibid., pp. 87-89.

CHAPTER SEVEN

QUESTIONS FOR REVIEW

1. List the ages of the Senior High student as well as the corresponding grades for the graded Sunday school.

2. In what way does physical fitness contribute to our spiritual well being?

3. Is the adolescent's knowledge factors any different than those of his forefathers? What does this mean to the Senior High teacher?

4. Why is the Bible I.Q. of many Sunday school scholars so low? What can be done about this problem?

5. Should the Senior High Sunday school teacher deal with such subjects as dating and marriage? If so, why? If not, why not?

6. Why does the public school have a distinct advantage over the Sunday school?

7. Do adolescents respond favorably to church attendance? To prayer? To Bible reading? To giving?

8. Discuss the lecture method. Consider the advantages and disadvantages.

9. Is the discussion method a good method to use with Senior High youth? Discuss your answer.

10. What advantages can be gained by using buzz sessions? Describe this method as fully as you can.

174

CHAPTER EIGHT

THE YOUNG ADULT STUDENT

You have now begun the last chapter in this book. It is not the last chapter in the spiritual maturation of the believer. This maturation continues on through one's life and is culminated at death or the second coming of Christ.

This chapter ought to be a volume. So little has been written about young adults and adults in the Sunday school that we can rightly say they are the neglected segment of Sunday school scholars. In these days of the large Sunday school class we follow the practice of grouping hundreds of a wide age variance into one giant Sunday school class. This may do well to reach the masses but it becomes difficult to make the Bible relevant to the needs of such a wide margin of ages. The young marrieds face far different problems than the social security set.

THE YOUNG ADULT'S MATURATION

This chapter will not follow the pattern of previous chapters for several very good reasons. By the time one becomes a Young Adult physical maturation is all but complete. Knowledge may be expanded by a college education but the basics of knowledge are already determined. The socialization of the Young Adult is nearly completed although every person will interact socially every day of his life.

The area of development that can continue on into the adult life is that of spiritual development. Every believer must continue to grow in the grace and knowledge of the Lord Jesus Christ. This growth process is begun with the new birth and continues through one's life. Some call the process sanctification. The Sunday school can and should make a strong contribution to this growth process. The Sunday school exists to evangelize the lost and edify the saved.

The Sunday school has the complex problem of teaching a complex Book. It is limited to one hour or less each Sunday. In this hour the Sunday school teacher must teach a portion of the Bible (the basic textbook of the Sunday school). The portion must be taught in light of the whole. The Bible must be (and can be) made relevant. The teacher has several things going for him. One is the Person of the Holy Spirit who will assist in the teaching program. The other is time. Though you only have one hour each Sunday you do have a multiple of Sundays for one never graduates from Sunday school.

The Young Adult. Grading by ages and school levels is completed at the Senior High level. The Young Adult is then thrust into a classroom situation that may or may not be to his advantage. Some churches provide for this age level with something like a "College and Career" class. Some churches divide the young marrieds from the young singles. Some churches resolve their problem of what to do with the Young Adult by retaining him with the Senior Highs or thrusting him into a class of adults. Usually he will not stay with either group but will become a Sunday school drop-out.

Today's Young Adult is now an adult. He is now recognized as an adult at age eighteen. He can vote and purchase his own liquor if he desires. The society he lives in has delayed his maturation by trying to retard his development on the one hand and yet spur his development on the other hand. He is asked not to "grow up" too soon and yet is given the privilege of voting, fighting for his country, and marriage without parental consent.

The Later Adolescent. The span of the years 18-24 are the years accredited to later adolescence by many psychiatrists. The Young Adult enters this age span as a high school senior or graduate. He enrolls in and completes his college education during these important years. He chooses his life-mate and begins his own family. He chooses his career. This is the age when three of the most important decisions of his life are made: college, career, and companion. This is a period of overlapping for some psychologists label this age as early adulthood, corresponding with middle and later adulthood.

THE YOUNG ADULT'S MOTIVATION

There is a great deal of activity today that is

designed to "turn the Young Adult on." The Young Adult is in the majority. All statistical surveys tell us that there are more people under thirty years of age than ever before in the history of the world. This is a young person's world. Fashions are designed with the Young Adult in mind. Entertainment is geared towards the Young Adult. It is during this age period that many young people turn to drugs and promiscuity.

Proper Motivation. Many years ago the Psalmist wrote, "This is the generation of them that seek him . . . " (Psalm 24:6). When the Young Adult reaches this age plateau he often finds his life is empty and void. This is especially true if he reaches this age without experiencing the new birth. When man lives apart from God he has a vacuum in his life. He becomes a part of the seeking generation. He tries to fill this vacuum with many things. He passes through life trying to fill this void with everything life affords him only to learn, sometimes too late, that only Christ can fill one's life and give one purpose.

The Young Adult Sunday school teacher can become a motivator as well as a teacher. This can be done by making the Word of God relevant. The Young Adult teacher should use a variety of methods in his teaching program and especially those that involve the pupil in class participation. Christ must be presented as the answer for He is the answer.

Improper Motivation. Too many Young Adults are

"turned off" by what they see and hear. Christ will not be meaningful to them if He is not meaningful to those who teach and lead Young Adults. If Sunday school is a dull and meaningless hour there will be little to motivate the Young Adult. On one particular Sunday the regular teacher did not appear to teach the Young Adult class. There were only four or five present for class. A substitute teacher was selected from the class. He readily admitted that he was unprepared to teach. It really didn't take the remaining class members long to discover this fact. What followed was a boring and meaningless class session where everyone read a paragraph or two and made a few comments. The class discussion was finished before the bell rang so they sat and talked about current events for the rest of the period. It is no wonder that only four or five attended this class. They were the brave ones.

Improper motivation can also take place outside of the church as well as inside. The Young Adult may not only decide to drop out of Sunday school and church but also society as well. Everyone is well acquainted with the hippie who has no motivation except for sex and drugs. These drifters can be seen along our nation's highways as they hitchhike to nowhere. They are like the western tumbleweed that breaks off and is tossed about listlessly by every wind that blows. The textbooks of the next generation will delve into the problems of the society drop-out.

THE YOUNG ADULT'S MATRICULATION

In the year of 1970 there were a total of 833,322 bachelor's degrees earned. In addition another 209,387 earned master's degrees while 29,872 earned doctorates. More young people are going to college now than ever before. In most instances vocational choices will determine college choices. Scholarships of several types may be the motivating factor in the choice of a college. Every state has huge universities that offer multi-field educational opportunities.

The Secular School. The majority of today's young people will decide to attend a secular college or university. Many select the college that is closest to home. The sixties spoke of revolution on almost every secular college campus. Buildings were burned, laws were broken, students were shot. The rebellion of the sixties has settled into a calm during the seventies.

The revolution has moved on even though it now moves more calmly. Coed dormitories are permitted on many campuses. The values that were established by the founding fathers of many institutions of higher learning are now gone. Evolution and social revolution are taught as facts of life. When the Young Adult Christian enrolls at a secular college or university he is subjecting himself to all types of attacks upon his faith. The strong Christian can withstand these assaults. The weak Christian may surrender to them.

The Christian College. The Christian Young Adult should strongly consider going to a Christian college. There are many excellent Christian schools across our nation. A Christian college is dedicated to promoting Christian values. This is done by carefully selecting a faculty that is committed to Christ. Academic standards are not allowed to override Christian standards. Many Christian colleges are called Bible colleges. A Bible college combines the curriculum of a liberal arts college with that of a seminary. The usual pursuit of a degree takes four years. In a Bible college every student is required to major in Bible although he may also major in another field at the same time.

Many Christian schools and Bible colleges are denominationally supported and affiliated. The Young Adult should consider attending one of the schools of his own denomination before he considers others.

The Young Adult teacher should point his pupils in the direction of the Bible college or Christian school. Every Sunday school scholar may not decide upon a church related vocation but he should attend such a school for at least two years. Most credits can be transferred to other institutions. During these first two years a good foundation of Bible knowledge and Christian convictions can be established.

THE YOUNG ADULT'S OCCUPATION

One of the great decisions of the youth years will

be, "How am I going to earn my living and support my family?" As has been stated the choice of a vocation will help determine the choice of a college.

Secular Vocations. Most Young Adults will enter secular fields of vocation. These vocations are now more varied and sophisticated than ever before. They can be taught to enter their particular field as Christians and to function as Christians in their chosen vocation. They can be instructed in the ways of serving God as one serves as employer.

Christian Vocations. For too long now one has thought that the field of full time Christian service was limited to the pastor, evangelist, or missionary. There are many and varied ways in which one may serve the Lord in a full time capacity. Here are just a few other than the three mentioned above:

1. Christian colleges and seminaries. There are many job opportunities that are open to those who are willing to prepare themselves for this type of service. Administrators and educators of these institutions are called of God to their specific vocation. They perform a valuable service for the Lord.

2. Christian nurseries and day schools. Many churches have begun day care centers and Christian day schools. It is difficult to find competent Christian teachers. Many Young Adults can be "pointed" in this direction.

3. Christian publishing. There are numbers of

excellent publishing houses that publish Christian literature of every description. There are job opportunities for editors, writers, typesetters, pressmen, etc.

4. Musical vocations. Some Young Adults can find rewarding experiences as a music director, organist, or pianist. Some churches employ musicians on a full time basis. Others have launched brilliant careers as a soloist or musician. The recording industry has brought financial rewards to many as well as being used as a means of spreading the gospel.

5. Christian education. Many churches hire a full time Christian Educational Director. Usually this person has earned his degree in the field of Christian education.

6. Denominational houses. Many denominations have headquarters of some sort that employ a broad field of talented people.

Through technical advance there will be other areas of service that one may render for the Lord. Every Young Adult should consider the Lord's will in the matter of vocational choice. God calls and then provides an open door of opportunity for service to those who respond to His call. As a motivator, the Young Adult teacher can help guide his pupils toward the Lord's will for their lives.

THE YOUNG ADULT'S MARRIAGE

One of the greater decisions that is made during the 18-24 span of years is that of a life-mate. Some adolescents make this decision early. The median age for marriage in America is now between 18 and 19 years for girls and age 21 for boys. Any marriage before that time is called an *early marriage*. Premarital pregnancy is the most common cause for high school students to marry. Others marry early because of problems at home or because of a romanticized concept of marriage and of the status that marriage gives. The tragedy of many of these early marriages is that they end in divorce.[2]

The Right Choice. Of course this section is directed to the teacher who is teaching a class of young single adults. You can be sure that each one in your class is concerned about marriage and is planning toward this move. In 1971 there were 22,629,000 single people in the United States who were over 18 years of age. Not all of these will marry but many of them will. The Christian young man should seek a Christian young lady for a mate and vice versa. The Bible is very explicit in its command, "Be ye not unequally yoked together with unbelievers: for what fellowship hath righteousness with unrighteousness? and what communion hath light with darkness?" (2 Corinthians 6:14). Paul surely had the yoke of marriage in mind when he penned these words.

The Wrong Choice. Many Christian young people have had their lives ruined by choosing the wrong person for marriage. Some young girl decides she can marry the young man who is not a Christian. She is "rather" sure she can win him to the Lord after she marries him. Then she spends the rest of her life praying for the salvation of her unsaved husband. This story has been told over and over again in many marriages.

The Young Adult Sunday school teacher can help in this vital decision. He doesn't have to be a match-maker but he can encourage the members of his class to "wait upon the Lord." Those who seek out the Lord's will in marriage will never regret their decision. Those who move ahead of the Lord often spend the rest of their lives in regret. As someone has said, "Marriage is a wonderful institution." Many young mis-matched couples fail to realize that they will have to spend their lives in the "institution" of marriage.

THE YOUNG ADULT'S MESSAGE

How old should one be before he starts to teach a Sunday school class? Some are pressed into service as a Sunday school teacher at an early age. We must keep in mind that a Sunday school teacher should be called of God. There are no age restrictions in God's program. He usually calls when we are ready to meet the demands that correspond to the call He extends to us.

The Young Adult As A Teacher. Many Young Adults have spent their lives in Sunday school. They are well versed in the Bible. God has spoken to a young lady about teaching a class of Preschoolers. There is no reason why she should not be permitted to teach if she is qualified. She should not be a novice. It would be best if she could gain some experience as an assistant teacher for a period of time. She should have completed at least some portion of teacher training and actively continue in such a program.

A young man of 19 has expressed a desire to teach a class of Junior boys. He is a new convert and has only been a member of the church for the past six months. Should he be encouraged to teach? The answer is obvious. He needs the Bible training he would normally receive in his own young adult Sunday school class. Each person must be judged upon his own merit. There is a list of requirements for every Sunday school teacher listed on page 72. Turn back and review this list now.

The Young Adult As A Witness. It was pointed out in chapter six that the Junior High student could be motivated to memorize Scripture to be used in witnessing for the Lord. The Young Adult student should be all the more ready to witness for Christ. The Young Adult teacher can take his class on witnessing missions. Services can be conducted, tracts can be distributed, and a faithful witness to the unsaved can be carried out.

THE YOUNG ADULT
IN RETROSPECT

One word can be used to describe the basic problems facing all Young Adults. That word is decision. Most Young Adults who attend Sunday school have already made their decision for Christ. They are faced with other major decisions. Where shall I go to school? What shall be my life's vocation? Whom shall I marry? The Young Adult cannot make these decisions alone and he does not have to. When his life is committed to Christ he can look to Christ for the answers. He can do so with the confidence that Christ has the answers.

THE YOUNG ADULT TEACHER

Challenge! Teaching Young Adults is a tremendous challenge and a rewarding experience. The Young Adult teacher must be more than a teacher; he must be a motivator. He must be this and possess all of the other qualities and qualifications that are outlined in the previous chapters of this book.

A VARIETY OF METHODS

It is time now to continue and complete our study that was introduced in chapter six. It would be well if you would review the material dealing with methods of teaching in the past two chapters. You will then be ready to complete this survey of methods.

Question and Answer. Every teacher has used the

Question and Answer method, if not in total, at least in part. The question and answer method is the active participation of the teacher and pupils in questions relative to lesson content and meaningful application to daily living. It is indeed the skillful use of questions that marks the good teacher. Dr. C. H. Benson says of teaching, "It is a probing process in which the surgical instrument is the question. The response of the pupil, like the recovery of the patient, will depend upon the skill with which the instrument is used."[3]

One of the most proficient users of the Question and Answer method was the Lord Jesus Christ. The four gospels record more than one hundred questions asked by Him. The Lord Jesus was a master of the art of questioning. At the age of twelve He was found asking questions (Luke 2:46). At the beginning of His public ministry He asked His first two disciples, "What seek ye?" This is typical of the thought-provoking and reflecting character of all His questions.

One important use of questions is to discover what the pupils do and do not know. The purpose may be to determine whether or not the pupil has mastered the essential facts in the lesson, but a better purpose is to test his understanding of these facts and his ability to use them in fruitful ways. A second use of the question is to aid the pupil to build upon his past experience. Third, the question arouses curiosity and stimulates interest. A few well-directed questions can change an apathetic student into an alert, interested one who is ready to undertake almost anything. Fourth, the question may be used to cause the pupil to think. By asking questions, the teacher brings problems and difficulties to the mind of the pupil and by further questioning he can lead the pupil to develop insight, see relationships, and organize his facts for purposes of definite accomplishment in working out a solution. A fifth use to which questioning may be put is that of directing attention to the significant elements in a situation or in materials.

With the Question and Answer method the teacher may choose to ask questions of the class and allow the class to ask questions in exchange. The teacher may choose to prepare a list of questions to ask and use the pupil's spontaneous answer as a springboard for his own discussion.

There are several types of questions that may be asked. One of these is contact questions. Attention and interest can be aroused if the teacher begins the lesson with an appropriate contact question. The most familiar and frequent expression of Jesus was, "What think ye?" Conversations were introduced by inquiries such as, "Will ye also go away?" "Whereupon shall we liken the kingdom of God?" and "Whence shall we buy bread that these may eat?"

Another type of question is the rhetorical question. Preachers and teachers often ask questions without expecting an answer. Such inquiries are asked for effect rather than reply. They occasion surprise and issue vital challenges. They stimulate mental activity.

Next, there is the factual question. These are questions that are answered by information previously given. The reply fixes in the mind the instruction that has already been imparted, and, since the work of a teacher is not complete until it has been tested, factual questions reveal how much instruction has reached its goal.

A fourth type of question is the thought-provoking question. Questions must do more than test the pupil's knowledge. They must help the pupil organize and apply his knowledge. They should stimulate the pupil to know more and to think for himself.[4]

Before the next method is presented there are some further observations about the Question and Answer method that should be made. Be sure to avoid questions that reveal the answer. Avoid guessing questions. When questions can be answered by "yes" or "no," the pupils will be tempted to guess rather than to think. Whenever a pupil gives a yes or no answer expect him to give a reason for his answer. Avoid long or double questions. Assign questions judiciously. (Never ask questions by alphabet or seating arrangements. This tends to alert the person next in line while the remainder of the class relaxes.) State the question before assigning it to the pupil. Answer questions with questions. Jesus did!

Research And Report. The methods previously discussed are the most popular in use today. By shifting methods the teacher injects variety into his teaching. These methods that have been discussed are not the only ones from which a teacher may choose. There are many more. In the space that is left we shall discover as many of these as we can.

One method that will prove interesting and involve several members of your group is the Research and Report method. With this method individual assignments are made. The researchers report their findings at a subsequent meeting. All assignments should be given at least one week in advance. Keep in touch with your researchers by telephone or visitation. The teacher will suggest possible resources for the class members to use for the research.

There are several rules that should be followed in making the assignments:

1. Be sure the pupil understands the assignment. Write it out if possible.

2. Provide necessary reference and source materials.

3. Always call for a report on the assignments.

4. Show sincere appreciation for achievements.

There are several types of research assignments that might be made. Some of these are:

1. A description of places or objects. A good Bible

dictionary will be valuable for this purpose.

2. A definition of words or scriptural terms. The pupil can use a regular dictionary as well as a Bible dictionary. He may wish to research some commentaries and theology books.

3. A third area of research is Word Study. Here the pupil will want to use a good concordance. By way of example the pupil might be asked to run a reference on the word "love" as it relates to God's love for man.

4. A fourth area of research could be the interview. Several pupils are sent forth to interview Christians in different walks of life regarding their opportunities for witnessing. Reports are then brought back to class. The interview might be used in other ways than the example given. Used appropriately it can be a valid form of research and report.

5. The researchers might be sent out to gather visual aids. These may include a large variety of things, from simple magazine pictures to missionary costumes.

The Research and Report method can be used for the entire class period or just a portion of the class period. It is an excellent instrument for introducing the lesson. Its value is evident. The pupils become involved as they participate in the research. They gain information and share it with their class members. The teacher should be careful so that the opportunities for research are shared by all members of the class.[5]

The Book Report. One valuable method of teaching is the Book Report. Almost every class member has had some experience in presenting book reports during the course of his public education.

The teacher will want to assign books that are related to the topic of discussion for the day. The teacher may choose to report on a book or books himself or he may make the assignment to others. There are many good books available and many can be purchased cheaply in paperback form. Some books that would be worthy of review would be biographies of Christians, especially great missionaries or preachers; topical books that deal with Christian principles; or doctrinal books that deal with Christian doctrines.

The Book Report is especially effectual for introducing some timely topic for the day. Unless it is an unusual book it should not occupy the entire class session.[6]

The Debate Forum. A very interesting method that some teachers might want to use is called the Debate Forum. With this method speakers are selected who have opposing views on a controversial subject. Each is given equal time to present the reasons for his beliefs. Time is allotted at the end of the session for the class to ask questions and participate in free and open discussion.

The teacher selects these debaters in advance and sets the rules for the debate. He arrives early and arranges the classroom setting which will call for a table with three chairs at the front of the classroom. The teacher will act as a moderator for the meeting and sit at the table with the debaters. Each debater will then present the issues and propositions within his allotted time. He will define terms and give adequate evidence of his viewpoints. He will attack the position of his opponent and defend his own position. This is to be done without becoming argumentative.

The teacher will open the session for free discussion after the debaters have completed their summarization. The class will then be guided into making a decision and arriving at conclusions as well as a course of action.

One can readily see that the Debate Forum should not be tried by the unskilled. If the debate becomes an argument the result could be disastrous. This disaster can be avoided by a trained teacher choosing experienced debaters. Some have gained this experience in high school or college debating. When this method is used properly it can be a most valuable method of teaching.

Projected And Non-Projected Visuals. The last method that we shall pay attention to is more of an aid to teaching than a method. It involves the projected and non-projected visual. The teacher may decide to use some appropriate film or filmstrip that would run the length of the time allotted for the class session.

The teacher may want to use a film or filmstrip for what is called a film talk-back. After a motion picture film or filmstrip is shown the teacher allows time for open discussion by the class members. The projected visual has been informative and the class members will want to express themselves accordingly.

There are several things the teacher should keep in mind when using the projected visual. If the film or filmstrip is to be rented or borrowed then the teacher should be sure of the scheduling of it. The teacher should have a working knowledge of the projection machine that he is to use. He should arrive early and have the machine ready to operate prior to the class session.

The teacher should not use the projected visual as a crutch for a lack of lesson preparation. It can be a valuable teaching aid or can be used in total as a method. It is to be used to complement the teacher's ministry and not to substitute for his ministry.

Non-projected visuals are such items as the chalkboards, bulletin boards, flannelgraph boards, puppets, objects, flat pictures, flip charts, posters, models, charts, and maps. Most of these will be used as aids to teaching and not become a method within themselves. However, the teacher with a sanctified imagination may utilize an aid as a method of presentation for the entire lesson. The teacher can adapt the aid or method that is most suitable for the age level of his class. Some items that might be considered childish by some can still be valuable in teaching adults. It will depend upon the skill of the teacher in using the aid or method.

In the same family with the projected and non-projected visual one will find some items that can be listed as audio aids. These are teaching aids which are heard such as the radio, records, tape recorders and cassette players. It would be difficult for the teacher to maintain the interest of the class for an entire class session by simply playing a recording or a cassette. The teacher could play a segment of a recording or cassette and pause for class discussion before going on to the next segment. This could be a very effective and useful method of teaching.

We have covered a multiplicity of methods in our discussion. The teacher may not be able to use each method in his teaching program. He will want to continue this research to discover methods that have not been mentioned. He should not use a method just because he does want to inject variety in his teaching but because it is the best and most logical way of presenting his lesson material. The wise teacher will make the choice of a method a matter of prayer and then follow the conscious leadership of the Holy Spirit.

We have learned that the use of methods in our teaching is scriptural. The Lord Jesus Christ injected a variety of methods into His teaching. He lectured; He used questions and answers; He did not hesitate to use an object lesson. In using a variety of methods we will be following the pattern established by the Savior.

CONCLUSION

The Young Adult teacher, like the Junior High and Senior High teachers, will use methods that involve their pupils. He will use a variety of methods so as to avoid the pattern of sameness in the Sunday school hour. This hour can become the most meaningful hour of the week. Boredom can be replaced by enthusiasm. Those who once endured Sunday school can now enjoy it.

CHAPTER EIGHT

FOOTNOTES

[1] William Lerner, director, *Statistical Abstract of the United States, 1972* (Washington, 1972), p. 133.

[2] Elizabeth B. Hurlock, *Adolescent Development* (New York, 1967), pp. 532-536.

[3] Clarence H. Benson, *Teaching Techniques for Sunday School* (Wheaton, 1963), p. 60.

[4] Ibid., pp. 61-62.

[5] Martha M. Leypoldt, *40 Ways To Teach In Groups* (Valley Forge, 1967), pp. 95-97.

[6] Ibid., pp. 39-40.

QUESTIONS FOR REVIEW

1. List the ages of the Young Adult or later adolescent.

2. What major decisions are made during this span of years?

3. Is it true that all young people seek after Christ? Explain your answer.

4. Discuss the importance of proper and improper motivation.

5. Why is it so important for the Young Adult to attend a Christian school? Explain.

6. Name some of the church related vocations that can be filled by today's Young Adults.

7. Why is it so important that a Christian Young Adult marry another Christian Young Adult?

8. Is it ever proper for a Young Adult to teach a Sunday school class? When?

9. Discuss the Question and Answer method. Be sure to list the types of questions.

10. Compile a list of projected and non-projected visuals.

EPILOGUE

The prologue of this book promised an exploration into the two facets that mold man into the creature that he is. These two facets are heredity and environment. The conclusion that we can contribute nothing to heredity of the offspring is correct. This is left to the genes and chromosomes of the parents and grandparents. It does help us to better understand an individual if we know something of his ancestorage. Our major problem is environment. We must provide a proper spiritual climate for our Sunday school scholars.

One can readily see from this text that Sunday school teaching involves teamwork. If one member of the team does not fulfill his role then the result can be disastrous. Each teacher deals with a child at a certain stage of his life and then passes that child on along to the next level. A portion of that teacher's life is invested in that child. The child's life might be compared to a chain. Each teacher is forging a link in that chain. The following poem describes the teacher's responsibility. The poet remains anonymous.

A builder builded a temple,
  He wrought it with grace and skill;
Pillars and groins and arches,
  All fashioned to work his will.
Men said as they saw its beauty,
  "It shall never know decay
Great is thy skill, o builder!
  Thy fame shall endure for aye."

A teacher builded a temple
　With loving and infinite care,
Planning each arch with patience,
　Laying each stone with prayer.
None praised her unceasing efforts,
　None knew of her wondrous plan,
For the temple the teacher builded
　Was unseen by the eyes of man.

Gone is the builder's temple
　Crumbled into the dust;
Low lies each stately pillar,
　Food for consuming rust.
But the temple the teacher builded
　Will last while the ages roll,
For that beautiful unseen temple
　Is a child's immortal soul.

The only correction that needs to be made to the above poem is the fact that there are more (than one builder) who are laying the stones.

We have covered more territory in our study than just pupil profiles. As a result we should have better tools to work with. If we understand the project we are working upon and if we have the proper tools we should be able to complete the task.

In some instances proper classroom settings are recommended. When the Sunday school complies and properly furnishes a room the teacher's task is made easier. In other instances teaching techniques are touched upon. There is much that the Sunday school teacher needs to know other than the Bible. In still other instances a variety of methods is suggested. Variety will always enliven anyone's teaching.

If you are a better teacher as a result of studying this book then every effort set forth to produce it has not been in vain. May God continue to call Sunday school teachers who will continue to prepare that His Word might continue.

BIBLIOGRAPHY

Avery, Marie L. and Alice Higgins, *Help Your Child Learn How To Learn.* New Jersey: Prentice-Hall, Inc., 1962.

Benson, Clarence H., *Teaching Techniques For Sunday School.* Wheaton: Evangelical Teacher Training Association, 1935.

Benson, Clarence H., *An Introduction To Child Study.* Chicago: Moody Press, 1942.

Blair, Arthur Witt and William H. Burton, *Growth And Development Of The Preadolescent.* New York: Appleton-Century-Crofts, Inc., 1951.

Carmichael, L., editor, *Manual Of Child Psychology.* New York: Wiley, 1954.

Caron, Ruth Shoule, *Juvenile Delinquency Development-Treatment-Control.* Philadelphia: J. B. Lippencott Company, 1969.

Crow, Lester D. and Alice Crow, editors, *Readings In Child And Adolescent Psychology. New York: David McKay Company, Inc., 1961.*

Gardner, D. Bruce, *Development In Early Childhood.* New York: Harper and Row, 1964.

Gregory, John Milton, *The Seven Laws Of Teaching.* Grand Rapids: Baker Book House, 1954.

Grinder, Robert F., editor, *Studies In Adolescence.* Toronto: The McMillan Company, 1963.

Hakes, J. Edward, editor, *An Introduction To Evangelical Christian Education.* Chicago: Moody Press, 1964.

Hurlock, Elizabeth B., *Child Development—Fourth Edition.* New York: McGraw-Hill, Inc., 1956.

Hurlock, Elizabeth B., *Adolescent Development.* New York: McGraw-Hill Book Company, Inc., 1955.

Jean, Frank Covert, and others, *Man And His Biological World.* Boston: Ginn and Company, 1944.

Lerner, William, director, *Statistical Abstract Of The United States,* 1972. Washington: United States Government Printing Office, 1972.

Leypoldt, Martha M., *40 Ways To Teach In Groups.* Valley Forge: The Judson Press, 1967.

McCandless, Boyd R., *Adolescents Behavior And Development.* Hinsdale: The Dryden Press, 1970.

Muuss, Rolf E., *Theories Of Adolescence.* New York: Random House, 1962.

Narramore, Clyde M., *How To Understand And Influence Children.* Grand Rapids: Zondervan, 1957.

Ruch, Floyd L., *Psychology And Life.* Chicago: Scott, Foresman and Company, 1948.

Soderholm, Marjorie Elaine, *Understanding The Pupil, Part I, The Preschool Child.* Grand Rapids: Baker Book House, 1967.

Soderholm, Marjorie Elaine, *Understanding the Pupil, Part II, The Primary and Junior Child.* Grand Rapids: Baker Book House, 1961.

Soderholm, Marjorie Elaine, *Explaining Salvation To Children.* Minneapolis: Beacon Publications, 1962.

Strickland, Hazel N. and Mattie C. Leatherwood, *Beginner Sunday School Work.* Nashville: Convention Press, 1955.

"Vocabulary," *The World Book Encyclopedia,* 1969, XIX, 337.

Willkens, William H. R., *The Youth Years.* Valley Forge: The Judson Press, 1967.

Zuck, Roy B. and Gene Getz, *Christian Youth, An In-Depth Study.* Chicago: Moody Press, 1968.